John Wesley's Concept of Sin

by

Leo George Cox, Ph.D.

Author of
John Wesley's Concept of Perfection

Published by Schmul Publishing Co.
PO Box 776
Nicholasville, KY 40340
USA

Printed in the United States of America

ISBN 10: 0-88019-453-7
ISBN 13: 978-0-88019-453-2

Visit us on the Internet at www.wesleyanbooks.com, or order direct from the publisher by calling 800-772-6657, or by writing to the above address.

Contents

Foreword **5**

1 Introduction **7**

The Purpose of This Book *8*
The Available Literature *9*
Wesley as a Protestant *11*
Sources of Wesley's Concepts *12*

2 Man Before the Fall **17**

His Creation *18*
His Body *19*
His Spirit *20*
His Natural Likeness to God *21*
His Moral Likeness to God *22*
His Perfect Law *24*
His Worth and Destiny *25*
His Liberty *25*

3 The Fall of Man **29**

The Origin of Sin *29*
The Account *30*
The Work of Satan *31*
The Nature of the First Sin *31*
The Consequent Loss *33*
The Threatened Penalty *35*
The Curse *36*

4 The Universality of Sin **39**

Wesley's View Before Georgia *39*
The Observation of the Indians *40*
The Influence of His Conversion Experience *41*
The Conflict with John Taylor *43*
Conditions Before the Flood *44*
Nature of Heathen Life *44*
Nature of More Civilized Man *45*
The Complete Corruption of Man *46*
Reasons for the Corruption *47*

5 The Transmission of Sin **50**

Taylor's Explanation *50*
The Headship of Adam *52*
The Imputed Guilt *53*
The Punishment for Original Sin *54*
The State of Infants *56*

5 The Transmission of Sin
Natural Generation ... 57
The Justice of God ... 58
The Natural Man ... 59

6 Prevenient Grace ... 64
Definition ... 64
Prevenient Grace Derived Through the Atonement ... 65
Benefits to the Race ... 66
Benefits to the Individual ... 69
Works Before Justification ... 70
All of Grace ... 71
Nature Plus Grace ... 72

7 The Nature of Sin—Willful ... 75
Definition ... 75
Personal Sin ... 78
Sin and Punishment ... 79
The Sins of the Unbeliever ... 79
The Willful Sin of the Believer ... 81
Repentance and Forgiveness ... 82

8 The Nature of Sin—Principle ... 85
Definition ... 85
The Root of All Sin ... 88
Sin in Believers ... 89
Repentance and Cleansing ... 90
Sin and Perfect Love ... 91

9 The Nature of Sin—Infirmity ... 95
Definition ... 95
Consequent to the Fall ... 97
Depravity of the Body ... 98
Lack of Knowledge ... 99
Wandering Thoughts ... 99
Mistakes ... 100
Sin and Temptation ... 101
Infirmity and Perfect Love ... 102
The Restored Image of God ... 103

10 The Influence of Wesley's View ... 107
The Summary of Wesley's Concept ... 107
The Development of Wesley's Views ... 108
Wesley's Influence in the Nineteenth Century ... 111
Wesley and the Twentieth Century ... 113
The Holiness Groups ... 114
The Methodist Church ... 115

Bibliography ... 123
The Writings of John Wesley ... 123
Supplementary Bibliography ... 123

Foreword

THIS PUBLICATION IS MADE available to us at a most appropriate time. A renewed antinomianism prevails in our evangelical culture. Many theologies have denied or ignored their biblical and historical roots, eventually losing their way in a fog of uncertainty on a sea of seductive speculation. Even many contemporary evangelical theologies fail to offer balanced and adequate foundations for an effective, holistic understanding and application of the liberating themes of the scriptural way of salvation. Wesley believed that a salvation message which did not proclaim the promise and power to restore the image of God's perfect love in the hearts of fallen men and women and set them to working in the prevailing culture is not the Gospel of *full salvation.* In evangelical thought and preaching today, just as in John Wesley's day, basic biblical teachings such as sanctification of heart and life, discipleship and spiritual discipline all too often have been diluted or relegated to the backwaters of Christian preaching and life. In such a time it is helpful to have a volume such as this which calls us back to the Scriptures and to Wesley's faithful coherence to them as a comprehensive whole.

Master's theses in theology, as in other areas of doctoral studies, commonly are a necessary exercise in the academic process and of interest only to the student and professor involved. Readers of this little volume will quickly learn that fortunately there are exceptions to that rule. The quality and potential usefulness of this thesis by the late Leo Cox proves that its writing has proved to be more than an exercise in fulfillment of requirements for his later dissertation on Wesley's concept of perfection. Drawing on the writings of Wesley's and his contemporaries along with relevant secondary sources, the author has given us not only a "master's thesis," but also a *masterful thesis.* It is a work that stands on its own. It constitutes a well-structured, well-reasoned, much-needed primer on many of the basic theological commitments that shape a biblical and Wesleyan understanding of God's plan of salvation.

The choice of title reveals the author's comprehensive grasp of Wesley's central theological concerns and how closely and consistently they support and relate to one another. One could adopt no more apt beginning point than Wesley's concept of sin to develop a review of what he believed to be a biblical theology of God's redemptive plan. Many years ago, during a brief interlude of bedside discussion with my father just before his premature death, he turned to me, a young and green theologian, and said, "Remember, if you're going to have an adequate biblical understanding of sanctification you'll have to have an adequate understanding of original sin." Dr. Cox takes us right to that question. He reminds us of Wesley's contention that a proper understanding of humankind's sinful nature constitutes the foundation for the whole of God's plan of salvation and that the belief in original sin marked a distinct dividing line between Christianity and heathenism. From there all else follows. Wesley's followers understood this. Wesleyan evangelists commonly noted that they first preached the law (of sin) so they could bring men and women to realize the fullness of grace.

This volume guides us and enlightens us at every step along that journey. It can help those who may not agree theologically with Wesleyans to understand them better. It can play an equally important role in helping his theological children to preserve and present their theological stance more effectively. For the sake of their own doctrinal and experiential integrity and for the benefit of all Christians, Wesleyans must understand the heart of their beliefs well enough to become loving but vocal critics of any contemporary teaching that ignores or limits the possibilities of grace and the potential of redeemed men and women to live holy lives as they share in God's redemptive plan.

—Melvin E. Dieter, Ph.D.
Professor emeritus,
Church History and Historical Theology
Asbury Theological Seminary

Chapter 1

Introduction

On the night of February 9, 1709, a lad of six years was by mistake left in the nursery on the second floor with the house on fire. The large Wesley family who resided in this parsonage in England had been aroused at eleven o'clock by one of the girls when fire began to fall on her bed. In the family's haste to escape John was left asleep. When he awakened, fire was all around him. He could not get out by way of the door or the stairway. He climbed upon a chest by the window and was seen by someone in the crowd below. A man standing on another's shoulders drew him from the window to safety just as the roof fell in. John Wesley, forty years later, looked back on this rescue with great thanksgiving.[1] He was looked upon as a "brand plucked out of the burning."[2] This lad grew to the man whose life's span touched every decade of the Eighteenth Century, and whose influence has been felt in every decade following.

Much has been written about this great man. This "brand out of the burning" has left an impact upon millions of people.

> With the possible exception of a few statesmen and scientists, perhaps a general or two, John Wesley has received more attention from the pen of biographers, and has had more written about him than any other Englishman of the eighteenth century. Time seems scarcely to have affected men's interest in him.[3]

However, most writers on Wesley have been interested in other phases of his life than his theology. "Naturally, the books about him are legion. The vast majority, however, treat him historically or from the point of view of religious psychology, comparatively few have subjected his theological position to scrutiny."[4] It is true that Wesley was a practical man and a leader of a great movement. These aspects of his life loom large in the popular mind. However, we must not overlook the fact that there is a theological basis for his message.

The Purpose of This Book

Most of the examination of Wesley's theological ideas has been confined to his teaching on perfection and justification by faith. His emphasis upon Christian experience, both in justification and sanctification, has been dealt with considerably in Methodism, and has been looked upon as the "primary idea of Methodism."[5] There has been much less work done on Wesley's idea of sin. It would be impossible to understand Wesley's concept of either justification or sanctification without first understanding his view of sin. It would not be possible according to Wesley to have a religious experience of salvation without first knowing the presence of sin.

> But no man can possibly "love his neighbor as himself," till he loves God, and no man can possibly love God, till he truly believes in Christ, and no man truly believe in Christ, till he is deeply convinced of his own sinfulness, guiltiness and helplessness. But this no man ever was, neither can be, who does not know that he has a corrupt nature.[6]

That Wesley considered the doctrine of sin to be of vital importance cannot be doubted. He lists the three "grand Scriptural doctrines" as "original sin, justification by faith, and holiness consequent thereon."[7] Holiness, for which he also used the terms *sanctification* and *Christian perfection,* was Wesley's main theme and for the propagating of this doctrine he believed the Methodists were especially called.[8] In his view the Reformers had ably taught the doctrine of justification by faith.[9]

Wesley placed the concept of man's sinful nature at the very foundation of the whole plan of salvation, and made acceptance of it all an essential mark of distinction between Christianity and heathenism.[10] No one can understand Wesley's teaching on sanctification without first seeking to comprehend his concept of sin. It is the purpose of this book to investigate this doctrine of sin as held by John Wesley.

It is hoped that this study may assist in the understanding of

Wesley's view on Christian perfection. It should also have a contribution to make in the contemporary trend in theological thought, which has placed a renewed emphasis upon original sin.[11] Since Wesley made his concept of sin so central in his thinking, since few theologians have made a thorough study of Wesley's doctrine of sin, and since there are conflicting opinions among them as to what Wesley did teach regarding sin,[12] a further study in this area of his thought is justified and desirable.

In order to carry out this purpose, it will be essential to examine Wesley's writings in detail. To know what his views were of man before the fall is important. How and why man fell, and what consequences such a fall had on the following generations are basic. Is sin for Wesley universal, and does God impute Adam's sin to all members of the human race? There is a need to discover his view of the natural man, of the "flesh", and of temptation. His various definitions of sin, and the distinctions he makes regarding the different aspects of sin will be noted.

Along with the investigation of Wesley's own writings will be a survey of the works of some writers who have made a special study of his theology. Some of these will agree, and some will disagree with Wesley. An attempt will be made to evaluate their comments in the light of Wesley's own view. A final comparison should then be made of Wesley's concept of sin with those concepts that have been and are now found in Methodism.

The Available Literature

Fortunately there are available many of Wesley's writings which he composed during his long life. Early in life he began to keep a journal in which he recorded many of his activities and reflections. The entirety of this journal is now available in *The Journal of the Rev. John Wesley* in eight volumes edited by Nehemiah Curnock. The *Journal* is also found in volumes three and four of *The Works of the Rev. John Wesley,* edited by John Emory. In this book most of the quotations from Wesley are taken from these *Works.*

Many of Wesley's theological ideas are found in his published sermons. In the seven-volume edition of Wesley's *Works,* edited by Emory, there are one hundred and forty sermons in volumes one and two. His *Standard Sermons,* edited by E. H. Sugden, appear in two volumes. Volumes five, six, and seven of Emory's edition contain miscellaneous writings including letters, treatises and some writings of other authors approved by Wesley. Many of his letters contain matters of theological interest, since they were often written to clear up misunderstandings on doctrine. His treatise, *The Doctrine of Original Sin According to Scripture, Reason, and Experience,* was written in answer to Dr. John Taylor, and is his most systematic treatment of any theological subject.

A very recent book entitled, *A Compend of Wesley's Theology,* compiled by Burtner and Chiles, is a systematic organization of some of Wesley's writings under various theological topics. This work contains some material not found in Emory's edition. Wesley prepared for his preachers a brief commentary on the New Testament. In this work, *Notes on the New Testament,* his opinions on various passages of the New Testament can be found.

Of the many secondary sources of material on Wesley, we shall mention only a few. Other works will be listed in the bibliography. John Fletcher, a contemporary of Wesley, and one of his leading Methodist preachers, sought to vindicate Wesley's teachings. His work, *Checks to Antinomianism,* is included in a four-volume set of his *Works* published in 1835.

In the Nineteenth Century there was a number of Methodist theologians who attempted to systematize Methodist theology. Two Englishmen, Richard Watson and W. B. Pope, wrote respectively the *Theological Institutes* and *Compendium of Christian Theology.* In America, Miner Raymond published his *Systematic Theology* in 1879, and John Miley's *Systematic Theology* appeared in 1892. R. S. Foster, also an American Methodist, published his six-volume set of *Studies in Theology* in 1899.

Two Twentieth-Century works that are representative of Wesleyan theology are *Fundamental Christian Theology* by A. M. Hills and *Christian Theology* by H. Orton Wiley. In these works there is the attempt to follow as closely as possible the theology of John Wesley, and of the Nineteenth-Century Methodist theologians.

A number of Twentieth-Century critical studies of Wesley's theology have been made. G. C. Cell in his *Rediscovery of Wesley* approaches Wesley from a Calvinist's point of view. In his book, *John Wesley in the Evolution of Protestantism,* Maximin Prette, a Roman Catholic, gives his criticism of Wesley's place in Protestant thought. Umphrey Lee discusses Wesley in the light of modern thought in his *John Wesley and Modern Religion.* J. Earnest Rattenbury and W.E. Sangster also have works on Wesley's theology.

The three most recent studies that are relevant to this present study have appeared in the last ten years [1957—*ed.*]. Harald Lindstrom, a Swedish theologian, wrote *Wesley and Sanctification* which is a study of the doctrine of salvation. In the book, *The Theology of John Wesley,* William R. Cannon deals specifically with the doctrine of justification. The third study is by George A. Turner entitled *The More Excellent Way.* He deals with "The Scriptural Bases of the Wesleyan Message."

Wesley as a Protestant

That Wesley has had a great influence upon the Protestant movement in the last two centuries can hardly be questioned. Lecky wrote that Wesley "has had a wider constructive influence in the sphere of practical religion than any other man who has appeared since the sixteenth century."[13] Protestantism owes much to John Wesley. He joined the succession of the Reformers when he became convinced of Luther's doctrine of justification by faith alone.[14] It was when he listened to the reading of "Preface" to Luther's *Commentary on the Romans* that he felt his heart "strangely warmed" and he knew he trusted in Christ alone for his salvation.[15] He thus adopted Luther's doctrine and remained faithful to it all his life. "It was the intellectual content of his Great Revival preaching. In this sense he was Luther's greatest son."[16]

Prior to the year 1738, when Wesley was thirty-five years old, there is little to indicate that he held to this basic Protestant principle. Both of his parents, who had repudiated their dissenting parents' Puritan positions, were faithful Anglicans. Their theology had been purged of its strong Puritan elements, and had become a form of "English Arminianism."[17] Being cradled as he was in the Church of England of the early Eighteenth Century, Wesley would not have imbibed very much directly from the Reformation thinkers.

A careful reading of his *Journal* from 1735, when he sets out for America, to 1738, in which year he dates his "conversion," reveals how far Wesley was from the teaching of the Reformers. He was an earnest seeker after salvation, but had little or no assurance of it. On his return from America he said in despair, "I went to America to convert the Indians, but Oh! Who shall convert me?"[18]

It was during this time, however, that he had his attention directed toward Luther. His contacts with the Moravians, and especially with Peter Bohler, convinced him of his need for faith and its assurance of salvation. It was in this setting he went to Aldersgate, and entered the experience that integrated his point of view. From this background Wesley launched forth into the revival that for Franz Hildebrandt was a "Revival of the Reformation."[19] Luther's influence on Wesley however became a "Reformation of the Revival."[20]

Sources of Wesley's Concepts

Toward the end of his life Wesley wrote,

> From a child I was taught to love and reverence the Scripture, the oracles of God, and next to these, to esteem the primitive fathers, the writers of the first three centuries. Next after the primitive church, I esteemed our own, the Church of England, as the most Scriptural National Church in the world."[21]

It is in this statement that we should find the key to the sources for Wesley's concept of sin.

There is no evidence that Wesley ever questioned the authority of the Bible. "In the year 1729, I began not only to read, but to study, the Bible, as the one, the only standard of truth, and the only model of pure religion."[22] In this sense Wesley held the Protestant position before 1738. His attitude toward the Scriptures was without doubt one reason why Bohler, and Luther, could find a ready listener in Wesley.

Even though Wesley lived at a time when some men laughed at

religion, and during the period of new attacks upon evangelical Christianity, he was not affected by them. He has little to say about the deistic controversies of the seventeenth and eighteenth centuries. His movement became a positive assertion of Christianity in the face of rationalism and deistic philosophy. Wesley believed in the powers of the mind and in reason. While others were using reason to attack revelation, Wesley used the power of his mind to explain and support the Word.[23] He believed reason needed the assistance of revelation.

Before Wesley's contact with the Moravians, there is no evidence that he held any other than the traditional view on the doctrine of sin. Since he was taught to hold in esteem the primitive church, and to reverence the Church of England, his acceptance of the Creeds and Articles was complete. That he did not fully grasp the Protestant significance of the *Thirty-Nine Articles* is clearly evident by his reactions after his "conversion" and his subsequent visit to Germany in the year 1738. It was following these events that he began "more narrowly to inquire what the doctrine of the Church of England is, concerning the much controverted point of justification by faith."[24]

Since the doctrine of justification by faith was a "new doctrine" to Wesley in 1738, one must not suppose that his doctrine of sin underwent a change at the same time. Up to that year Wesley had been in earnest pursuit of holiness. Three writers had greatly influenced him in his early college days—Thomas à Kempis, Jeremy Taylor, and William Law. Taylor convinced him that all his labors and services were to be directed toward God. After reading *The Imitation of Christ,* Wesley set out to pray an hour or two every day. William Law led him to pledge himself to love God perfectly.[25]

Although reading of these three men did not lead Wesley to the doctrine of justification by faith alone, it is clear that they would not have led him away from the traditional concept of sin. Each of them recognized the corruption of man's nature, and the need for a change of life.[26] By them Wesley was inspired to holiness of heart and life and to a severe, spiritual discipline because of inner sinfulness, but they did not lead him to Christian assurance.

Nor is there evidence that the contemporary teaching of the Church of England in Wesley's youth would have led him to question the traditional view on sin. In the Eighteenth Century the doctrine of sin was more ignored than attacked or rejected.

> After the time of Locke it is hard to find either orthodox or deist thinkers of England concerning themselves with the doctrines of the fall or original sin. In most of the theological treatises of the time, the subject is scarcely mentioned.[27]

An exception to this was the controversy aroused by John Taylor's attack on original sin published in 1746, to which later reference will be made.

The English Church of the Sixteenth Century laid a solid foundation for Protestant teaching in the *Thirty-nine Articles,* the *Homilies,* and the *Prayer Book.* Richard Hooker had great influence in formulating this interpretation of Protestant doctrine, but he was not prepared to go all the way to Geneva in his theology. Though no lover of Calvinistic discipline, "he still had a high respect for its theology. He left man helpless in his sinfulness and consistently refused to set any conditions on the divine bestowal of grace…"[28]

It cannot be said that the later divines of the Church of England rejected the *Articles.* Bishop Bull, whose writings influenced the mother of Wesley,[29] claimed to follow the *Articles* but, along with others, used his own interpretations.[30] However far he may have gone from the Reformers in his view on other doctrines, there is no indication that Bishop Bull's concept of sin differed greatly from theirs. "Nor did the High Church Arminianism in which Wesley was trained teach the natural religious or moral ability of man. Arminianism was a doctrine of grace, presuming original sin in man."[31]

That this stern concept of sin was impressed upon Wesley in his home is very evident. It was his privilege to be born into a home of great piety and of intelligent discipline. His mother had been a Socinian at an early age, but was drawn back into orthodoxy by her husband and Bishop Bull.[32] In his home Wesley was taught well the doctrines of the Church found in the *Articles* and in the Bible. An example of how Susanna Wesley regarded her children appears in a letter written to her fourteen-year-old daughter.

> I cannot tell whether you have ever seriously considered the lost and

> miserable condition you are by nature. If you have not it is high time to begin to do it, and I shall earnestly beseech the Almighty to enlighten your mind ...[33]

It is possible to conclude that Wesley never had a change of opinion in his concept of sin, as he did in his concept of justification by faith. However, there is evidence that he clarified and intensified his idea of sin through the years of his ministry, He was forced into controversial writings because of the opposition to his doctrine of Christian perfection. In these controversies with the Moravians, with the Calvinists, and with John Taylor, Wesley was forced to define his concept of sin, and to draw various distinctions. It is in these definitions and distinctions that we find his most clear and mature thoughts on the doctrine of sin.

In the attempt to make a systematic analysis of Wesley's concept of sin, it is well to keep three factors clearly in mind. First, with this background of his thought that has just been suggested, and with this account of his experiences that placed him in the line of the Protestant succession, one can expect Wesley to hold in general to the traditional Augustinian-Protestant view of original sin. Second, since he has an Arminian leaning and opposes predestination, Wesley will be found to differ from the Reformers in his definition of sin as related to God's grace and man's freedom. Third, Wesley's special teaching on Christian perfection requires him to distinguish amongst the various degrees of sin as found in the believer and in the entirely sanctified person. With these factors in mind we shall now pursue the examination of Wesley's concept of the doctrine of sin.

Endnotes

1. *The Works of the Rev. John Wesley,* compiled by John Emory, 3 ed., New York: The Methodist Book Concern, 1831, III, 475.
2. *Ibid.,* VII, 415 .
3. William Cannon, *The Theology of John Wesley,* New York: Abingdon-Cokesbury Press, 1946, 13.
4. Harald Lindstrom, *Wesley and Sanctification,* London: The Epworth Press, 1946, I.
5. W. J. Townsend, *A New History of Methodism,* London: Hodder and Stoughton, 1909, I, 7.

6. *Works,* V, 575.
7. *Ibid.,* VI, 757.
8. *Ibid.,* II, 389.
9. *Ibid.,* VII, 154.
10. *Ibid.,* I, 398.
11. James Spalding, *Recent Restatements of the Doctrine of the Fall and Original Sin,* Ann Arbor: University Microfilms, 1950, 2.
12. George Turner, *The More Excellent Way,* Winona Lake: Light and Life Press, 1952, 14. (Now available from Schmul Publishing Co., Nicholasville, KY.)
13. W. E. H. Lecky, *A History of England in the Eighteenth Century,* New York: D. Appleton and Company, 1879, II, 687.
14. *Works,* III, 66.
15. *Ibid.,* 74.
16. Ernest Rattenbury, *The Conversion of the Wesleys,* London: The Epworth Press, 1938, 183.
17. Cannon, *op. cit.,* 45.
18. *Works,* III, 55.
19. Franz Hildebrandt, *From Luther to Wesley,* London: Lutterworth Press, 1951, 110.
20. *Ibid.,* 159.
21. *Works,* VII, 325.
22. *Ibid.,* VI, 848.
23. Cannon, *op. cit.,* 15-16.
24. *Works,* III, 113.
25. Cannon, *op. cit., 57.*
26. Thomas à Kempis, *The Imitation of Christ,* New York: J. M. Dent and Sons, 1910, 180, 208, 216-218. William Law, *A Serious Call to a Devout and Holy Life,* New York: E. P. Dutton and Co., 1906, 12, 334-335. Jeremy Taylor, *Holy Living and Holy Dying,* London: Henry G. Bohn, 1850, 234.
27. Spalding, *op. cit.,* 44-45.
28. Cannon, *op. cit.,* 35.
29. *Ibid.,* 44.
30. *Ibid.,* 87.
31. Umphrey Lee, *John Wesley and Modern Religion,* Nashville: Cokesbury Press, 1936, 120-121.
32. Cannon, *op. cit.,* 43-44.
33. Original not available for examination, cited in Abram Lipsky, *John Wesley, a Portrait,* New York: Simon and Schuster, 1928, 23.

Chapter 2

Man Before the Fall

WESLEY PUT NO BOUNDS on the desire for knowledge. Man wants to know and is not satisfied until he ascends "to the source of all knowledge, and all excellence, the all-wise, and all-gracious Creator." However, although the desire has no bounds, the actual knowledge has. It is confined to narrower limits than the common man realizes, or the men of learning are willing to acknowledge. This lack of knowledge befits our present state, and our knowledge of the Creator or of his works is amazingly small.[1]

How then can we know anything about the first man? Certainly man cannot know by speculation or innate processes of the mind. Wesley believed man could know only by the senses unless God would reveal truth in a special way.[2] Man can know some things by observation of the world around him. He writes in his *Compendium of Natural Philosophy,* "But the book of nature is written in a universal character, which every man may read in his own language. It consists not of words, but things which picture out the Divine Perfections."[3] In the "Preface" to this work, he writes,

> It will be easily observed, that I endeavor throughout, not to account for things, but only to describe them. I undertake barely to set down what appears in nature, not the cause of those appearances. The facts lie within the reach of our senses and understanding, the causes are more remote. That things are so, we know with certainty, but why they are so, we know not. In many cases we cannot know, and the more we inquire, the more we are perplexed and entangled. God has so done his works, that we may admire and adore, but we cannot search them out to perfection.[4]

Wesley's account of the first man and his fall, and of man in general, will be guided by sense observations which will be very limited, and by what is found in the Bible and interpreted by reason. Man cannot know God, until God reveals Himself, the "veil of flesh" hides God from man, no man can know unless God reveals.[5] But to understand this revelation, one must use reason. "It is by reason that God enables us, in some measure, to comprehend his method of dealing with the children of men, the nature of his various dispensations, of the old and new covenant, of the law and the gospel." This use of reason is not "reasonings" or "imaginations," but simply reason assisted by the Holy Spirit, and enabling us to understand the Scriptures.[6]

His Creation

On this basis, then, God is known to be the Creator of heavens and the earth. He is revealed under a two-fold character—as Creator and Governor. As Creator, he acts under his own sovereign will, as Governor, according to justice and mercy.[7] As Creator of all things, he is also Preserver, so therefore has concern for all things and men. He will never forget his creation.[8] From the lowest to the highest, there is a gradual ascent, so that transitions from one species to another are almost insensible. There is an infinitely greater space between man and God, than between man and the lowest creature.[9]

But Wesley will not have it that present observations of the world tell us what it was like when God created it. All the "cavils of minute philosophers" and the objections of "vain men" who question God's goodness because of the present condition of the earth are based upon a false assumption. "The world at the beginning was in a totally different state from that wherein we find it now."[10] Since it was different, what was its condition? Wesley draws all his inferences from the Bible.

"And God saw that it was good." In this sentence God gives approbation to his works. They are good in every particular. The matter of the heavens and the earth was made of four elements—earth, water, air, fire, all mingled together. The earth was good; there were no deformations. It was beautiful, fertile, and not jagged and rough. There were no earthquakes, volcanoes, violent winters or sultry summers. All elements combined together for the welfare and pleasure of man.[11]

There was beautiful vegetation, with no weeds or poisonous plants. Among the animals there was no attempt to devour, nor harm; all was peaceful and quiet. The spider was harmless as the fly; even the reptiles were harmless and intelligent.

> Such was the state of creation, according to the scanty ideas which we can now form concerning it, when its great author, surveying the whole system at one view, pronounced it "very good!" It was good in the highest degree whereof it was capable, and without any mixture of evil. Every part was exactly suited to the others, and conducive to the good of the whole. There was "a golden chain," to use the expression of Plato, "let down from the throne of God," an exactly connected series of beings, from the highest to the lowest; from dead earth, through fossils, vegetables, animals, to man, created in the image of God, and designed to know, to love, and to enjoy his Creator to all eternity.[12]

Wesley believed the animals have an "innate principle of self-motion," a degree of understanding, and a will, which he defines as various passions. They have liberty—a power of choice. In their kind, these qualities were perfect in the beginning. There is a barrier between man and the beast. It is not reason or understanding, for beasts have such. But they are not capable of knowing and loving God. Here is the essential difference between man and the brute. Man and beasts were both immortal.[13]

Adam is the first man, and all are descendants of him.[14] In some sense he is head and representative of the whole race.[15] Are there other worlds with people? Wesley does not know. He thinks it may be possible, but not likely.[16] He is particularly concerned with Adam and the human race he begins.

His Body

The body of man was ever of interest to Wesley. Its composition, life, heat, breathing, blood circulation—all raised questions in his mind. What is muscle? What are animal spirits? What is dreaming? He admits it is very little we know.[17] The body is made of "dust," yet made wonderfully into "fibers, nerves, membranes, muscles, arteries, veins, vessels of various kinds." In it there is a mixture of fire with earth, air and water.[18] It has a wonderful heart and is a "curious machine" that is "fearfully and wonderfully made."[19]

In its original state the human body was not liable to pain or death, yet it needed the continual sustenance of food. Although it was not liable to weariness, yet it needed sleep for rest.[20] There was no harm that could befall the body. It was to be governed by the soul although there were the involuntary actions within the body.[21] The body is a gift of God to man with all its organs of sense, but it belongs to God and should be employed according to his will.[22]

In this body before the fall, man had a greater degree of strength and swiftness. He had an understanding beyond any successor. He saw with unspeakable pleasure all the beauty and harmony of creation. There was no evil to mar his pleasure; there was no sorrow or pain. While he was yet innocent, he was happy and he was impassive—incapable of suffering. "Nothing could stain his purity of joy. And to crown all, he was immortal."[23] Such a body according to Wesley did Adam possess.

His Spirit

Man was not merely a lump of earth, "a clod of earth," without sense or understanding. He was created a spirit like his Creator. As such he had sense, understanding, will and liberty. This spirit is clothed with a material vehicle.[24] The soul is a spirit, but we know very little about it. Where is it located? How is it connected to the body? Wesley does not know.[25] He thinks it may be located in some part of the head, but he cannot be certain.[26] That there is a spirit he is sure.

The body is not the man. He is an immortal spirit. He is "a spirit made in the image of God; an incorruptible picture of the God of glory; a spirit that is of infinitely more value than the whole earth. Of more value than the sun, moon and stars, put together, yea, than the whole material universe." It is of a higher order, of a more excellent nature and more endurable.[27] Wesley finds in himself something that "thinks," "judges," and "reasons." It reflects upon its own actions and is endued with imagination and memory.[28]

Is there any difference between soul and spirit? In commenting upon Paul's statement in I Thessalonians 5:23, where Paul uses the terms *spirit, soul, and body.* Wesley sees a problem. He says soul must be either material or immaterial because there is no medium. Spirit is the highest principle in man made in God's image, and endued with self-motion, understanding, will and liberty. The body is the organized matter received in the womb. It is connected with flesh and blood, but these are not the body. They are only temporary clothing of the body. The soul is the "immediate clothing of the spirit, the vehicle with which it is connected from its first existence, and which is never separated from it, either in life, or in death." It may be "ethereal or electric fire, the purest of all matter" and will never undergo any essential change.[29]

It is only by faith that man can know he is a spirit.[30] This spirit, made equal to the angels, cannot be satisfied on material things. It must have the fruit growing in the paradise of God.

His Natural Likeness to God

Wesley often uses the term *in the image of God.* What does he mean by it? He distinguishes three images—natural, political, and moral. The *natural image* is a picture of immortality, a spiritual being endued with understanding, freedom of will and various affections. The *political image* gives man dominion over all the lower things of the earth. But chiefly Wesley believes the image to be *moral.* Man is like God in "righteousness and true holiness," in love, in justice, mercy and truth. This is what is meant when God pronounced man to be "very good."[32]

Although Wesley uses the term *political image* in the above passage as distinct from the *natural image,* in other places it is combined with the natural image as being the same. The natural image relates to man's better part, his spirit, and as a spirit he is like God. As spirit and like God he has understanding, which seems to be the most essential property of spirit. In this unfallen state, Adam probably discerned truth by intuition. He was able to name every creature, as soon as he saw it, according to its nature. Since he was a creature, his knowledge would be limited, and he could be ignorant, but it does not appear that he was ever mistaken. However, he could be deceived.[33]

Adam was also endued with a will. By will, Wesley meant various affections, such as love, desire and delight in the good. He said man's soul is capable of love, hatred, joy, sorrow, desire, fear, hope, and a "whole train of other inward emotions, commonly called passions or emotions. They are styled, by a general appellation, the will; and are mixed and diversified a thousand ways."[34]

By natural image, then, Wesley meant man's equipment as a spiritual being. He had understanding, which he also called reason with all of its perfections.[35] He had the power of self-motion. He had the power of will which included the emotions and affections. He also had liberty which is free will in the sense of freedom of choice. This was man's "original nature" as it came from God's hand. For modem psychology, "original nature means man's uneducated equipment, his nature independent of postnatal nurture."[36] What the psychologists now mean by it, Wesley called "our present corrupt nature" as we shall later see.

Sugden in explaining Wesley distinguishes two elements in the divine image in man,

> (1) the natural image, including what is here called the political—that is, the mental constitution of man, his reason and power to apprehend truth, in virtue of which he is able to master and control the lower animals and make the forces of nature subservient to his needs; and (2) the moral image, the knowledge of right and wrong, and the capacity for fellowship with God.[37]

His Moral Likeness to God

What is this moral image of God in man? Dr. Pope, a close student of Wesley, remarks, "The distinction between the image that was indestructible, and that which might be lost has an unqualified and necessary truth."[38] Wesley calls this moral image the right state of the intellectual powers and love which is true holiness.[39]

> In this image of God man was made. "God is love:" accordingly, man at his creation was full of love; which was the sole principle of all his tempers, thoughts, words and actions. God is full of justice, mercy, and truth. So was man as he came from the hands of his creator. God is spotless purity; and so man was in the beginning pure from every sinful blot; otherwise God could not have pro-

> nounced him, as well as all the other works of his hands, "very good." Genesis 1:31. This he could not have been, had he not been pure from sin, and filled with righteousness and true holiness. For there is no medium; if we suppose an intelligent creature not to love God, not to be righteous and holy, we necessarily suppose him not to be good at all; much less to be "very good."[40]

This "Adamic perfection" made Adam as free from sin as the holy angels. His understanding was clear, so he could always judge right and thus always be able to speak and act right.[41] This acting right was preceded by a state of purity or holiness. There is a right state and a right use of all his faculties.[42] Wesley believed this moral image could be restored in the believer even though the perfection of Adam could not in this life. In referring to such texts as Colossians 3:8-12 and Ephesians 4:22, 24 where the believer is to put on the new man, "which is renewed in knowledge after the image of him that created him" and "which is created after God in righteousness and true holiness," Wesley sees the picture of the original moral image. He says, "These texts (along with others of Paul), therefore, do manifestly refer to personal, internal holiness; and clearly prove, that this is the chief part of that 'image of God' in which man was originally created."[43]

Further evidence that Wesley distinguished between right state and right action is found in his controversy with John Taylor. When Taylor argues that "righteousness is right action," Wesley answers,

> Indeed it is not. Here (as we said before) is your fundamental mistake. It is a right state of mind, which differs from right action, as the cause does from the effect. Righteousness is, properly and directly, a right temper or disposition of mind, or a complex of all right tempers.

He claims that love of God is righteousness, and must exist in the soul before it can be applied to action. However it was not irresistible.[44]

To understand Wesley here one must observe two fundamental distinctions. There is a distinction between the possibility to holiness and holiness itself. The first is a negative state, and the latter is a positive attitude of soul which inclines one to obey the right and reject the wrong. This latter is what Wesley means by holiness in Adam. The second distinction is between created holiness and ethical holiness. The first is a state of the mind while the latter is action which involves responsibility. The moral image in Adam would be the former, the created holiness. Ethical holiness, on the other hand, would be any right action that springs from moral choice.[45]

His Perfect Law

Adam was placed under a perfect law according to his ability. Since he was made holy, pure, merciful and perfect, even as God is, "God gave him a perfect law, to which he required full and perfect obedience." This obedience was to be performed without any intermission from his creation until his trial was over. No allowance was made for any falling short nor was there need for any. Man was "altogether equal to the task assigned, and thoroughly furnished for every good word and work."[46]

This "perfect law" was much more than is required of fallen man. It was more than loving God with all the heart, which was only a part of that law. Adam's ability was such, with both the perfect natural image and the moral image of God, that he could keep this law. His law was far wider than ours as his faculties were more extensive.[47] This Adamic law given to him is called the law of works.

> This is in substance the same as the angelic law, being common to angels and men. It required that man should use, to the glory of God, all the powers with which he was created. Now, he was created free from any defect, either in his understanding or affections. His body then was no clog to the mind; it did not hinder his apprehending all things clearly, judging truly concerning them, and reasoning justly, if he reasoned at all. I say, *if he reasoned;* for possibly he did not. Perhaps he had no need of reasoning, till this corruptible body pressed down the mind, and impaired its native faculties. Perhaps, till then, the mind saw every truth that offered as directly as the eye now sees the light.[48]

This perfect law includes the moral law that was written on the hearts of all men when they came from the hands of the creator. It is in force upon all mankind and in all ages. It is founded on an unchangeable relationship between God and man. Christ, the second Adam, came and fulfilled every part of this moral law. It is included in that religion which is as old as the human race, and was given to man when he "became a living soul."[49]

His Worth and Destiny

Man is of great worth. Since he is made in the image of God, he is of untold value. Wesley recognizes the tremendous magnitude of God's creation, and sees the smallness of man in relation to it, and wonders why God would recognize so "diminutive a creature." When he considers duration and how short the time is that man is on earth compared to the eternal God, he can ask, Why should God take any knowledge of him? But since man is a spirit that will live forever, he is of great worth. Of course the greatest reason to believe that God highly regards man is that he sent his son to die for him after he had sinned against God and lost his first estate.[50]

For what end did God make man? Why did God put man on the earth? Wesley answers, "For one sole end, and for no other, to prepare for eternity." And what was the end of his creation? "It was one and no other,—that he might know, and love, and enjoy, and serve his great Creator to all eternity." That "end" has not changed, even though man has sinned.[51]

> He "made all things," as the wise man observes, "for himself:" "for his glory they were created." Not "as if he needed anything;" seeing "he giveth to all life, and breath, and all things." He made all things to be happy. He made man to be happy in himself. He is the proper centre of spirits; for whom every created spirit was made. So true is that well-known saying of the ancient fathers… "Thou hast made us for thyself: and our heart cannot rest till it resteth in thee."[52]

Thus it can be seen, that in Wesley's opinion, man is of great value in the eyes of God. His destiny is of such great importance that all man's powers should be exercised to attain it.

His Liberty

God made man with "liberty" which is a power of directing his own affections and actions, and a capacity for determining his own choice.

All other powers of man would have been of no use had man not this power of free choice.[53] It is evident that Wesley means by his term *liberty* nothing more or less than the common acceptance of the word "will."[54] Man was free to choose his destiny. There was no law of necessity on him. Adam was free to choose either good or evil.[55]

Unless a man were a free agent he would be no agent at all. If liberty is necessitated, it is really no liberty at all. It is the same as "unfree freedom" which is downright nonsense. In fact, according to Wesley, where there is no liberty there can be no moral good or evil.

"There is no virtue, but where an intelligent being knows, loves and chooses what is good; nor is there any vice, but where such a being knows, loves and chooses what is evil." Could Adam choose evil, knowing it to be evil? Probably not, according to Wesley, but he could mistake evil for good. "He was not infallible; therefore, not impeccable. Sin came then by the abuse of man's liberty."[56]

Endnotes

1. *Works*, I, 116-117.
2. *Ibid.*, III, 406.
3. Burtner and Chiles, *A Compend of Wesley's Theology*, New York: Abingdon Press, 1954, 30.
4. *Works*, VII, 579.
5. *Ibid.*, V, 140.
6. *Ibid.*, II, 125-128.
7. *Ibid.*, VI, 135
8. *Ibid.*, II, 102
9. Burtner and Chiles, *op. cit.,* 35-36.
10. *Works*, II, 30.
11. *Ibid.*, 25-27.
12. *Ibid.*, 28-29.
13. *Ibid.*, 51.
14. *Ibid.*, 103.
15. *Ibid.*, V, 508-509.
16. *Ibid.*, II, 367.
17. *Ibid.*, 120-121.
18. *Ibid.*, 33.

19. *Ibid.*, 402 .
20. *Ibid.*, 27.
21. *Ibid.*, II, 403.
22. *Ibid.*, I, 450.
23. *Ibid.*, II, 50-51.
24. *Ibid.*, 31-36.
25. *Ibid.*, 120.
26. *Ibid.*, 403.
27. *Ibid.*, 366.
28. *Ibid.*, 402-403.
29. *Ibid.*, VI, 532-533.
30. *Ibid.*, II , 407.
31. *Ibid.*, 453.
32. *Works*, I, 400.
33. *Ibid.*, II, 69.
34. *Ibid.*, 403.
35. *Ibid.*, 127.
36. John Prince, *Wesley on Religious Education*, New York: Methodist Book Concern, 1926, 19.
37. E. H. Sugden, *Standard Sermons* by Wesley, London: Epworth Press, 1921, I, 227-228.
38. William B. Pope, *A Compendium of Christian Theology*, New York: Hunt and Eaton, 1889, I, 424.
39. *Works*, V, 561.
40. *Ibid.*, I, 400.
41. *Ibid.*, II, 168.
42. *Ibid.*, II, 50.
43. *Ibid.*, V, 594-595.
44. *Ibid.*, 596-597.
45. H. Orton Wiley, *Christian Theology*, Kansas City: Nazarene Publishing House, 1941, II, 41.
46. *Works*, I, 45.
47. *Ibid.*, VI, 739.
48. *Ibid.*, 512.
49. *Ibid.*, I, 222.
50. *Ibid.*, II, 364-368.
51. *Ibid.*, 405.

52. *Ibid.*, 430.
53. *Ibid.*, 31.
54. Prince, *op. cit.*, 17-18.
55. *Works*, VI, 127.
56. *Ibid.*, II, 69-70.

Chapter 3

The Fall of Man

MAN DID NOT KEEP his first estate. He fell and thus brought sin into the world. How can one know these facts to be true? Wesley, as has been noticed, judged all things by the "Oracles of God." He found his description of man's original state in the Bible; it is there he finds the account of the fall. In fact man could never have discovered with all the wisdom he possessed the simple account of the origin of evil, had God not been pleased to reveal it. And this "plain, simple account" is given to us in Genesis, chapter three, and in a "full and satisfactory" manner. This manner "does not indeed serve to gratify vain curiosity," but is abundantly sufficient to "justify the ways of God with men."[1]

The Origin of Sin

How did Wesley consider that a holy being could sin? Why would this man created in the image of God and inclined to the good, full of love, fully happy, ever turn from such a way? To be a holy and moral being with intelligence man must be free. He needed this liberty even to be holy or to have any kind of virtue. The same freedom that enabled him to be holy also enabled him to choose the wrong. So actually sin entered by the wrong use of his God-given freedom.[2]

> It must be admitted that Wesley gives no adequate explanation of the origin of sin: he does not show how a righteous nature can itself generate unrighteousness, or how that which was made good and upright can convert itself into evil. But he does affirm that sin arose as the creative and independent act of man's own nature, that it emerged as the result of free choice, and that God cannot be blamed with its existence.[3]

Whether Wesley's account of the origin of sin is "adequate" for other theologians or not, it was satisfactory to Wesley's mind. He claims this liberty in man "necessarily included a power of choosing or refusing either good or evil." He says some have doubted whether man could choose evil knowing it to be evil. But he "might mistake evil for good. He was not infallible; therefore, not impeccable." And for Wesley, this "unravels the whole difficulty of the grand question, 'Unde malum?' "How came evil into the world?"'"[4]

The Account

In Wesley's exposition of the third chapter of Genesis he begins suggesting that the serpent may have been endowed with reason before the fall. Unless he were able to reason and thus to speak, why was not Eve surprised or startled when the animal spoke? Yet she shows no surprise and enters into conversation with him. She remains clear of any blame until she begins to believe the serpent's word rather than God's. "Here sin begins, namely, unbelief... She believed a lie, she gave more credit to the word of the devil, than to the word of God. And unbelief brought forth actual sin."[5]

To deceive Eve, Satan—as Wesley calls the serpent—mingled falsehood with truth and thus persuaded her to disbelieve God. She laid herself open to the whole temptation. This temptation included "the desire of the flesh," "the desire of the eyes," and "the pride of life." This "unbelief begot pride," and she thought herself wiser than God; "it begot self-will," so she determined to do her own will; "it begot foolish desires," so she partook of the forbidden fruit.[6]

Eve was deceived according to the apostle, but Adam was not. How then did he join in the sin? "She gave unto her husband and he did eat." He sinned with his eyes open. "He rebelled against his Creator, as is highly probable,— 'not by stronger reason moved, but fondly overcome with female charms. '"Adam first sinned in his heart even before he ate. This was inward idolatry—loving the creature more than the creator.[7] He wilfully and openly rebelled against God, and cast off his allegiance to the majesty of heaven."[8] He would not be guided by the Holy Spirit; he would be wise in his own way and in his own strength. He "did not depend in simplicity upon his heavenly Father."[9] By this act of Adam and his wife, Eve, sin came into the world.

The Work of Satan

As was noticed in the last section, the serpent who beguiled Eve is called Satan. This beginning of sin is called by Wesley the "work of the devil." In fact sin began with the devil who was "Lucifer, son of the morning." The devil who "sinneth from the beginning" was the first to sin in the universe. He introduced sin into creation by the abuse of liberty and so he is the author of sin. He was "self-tempted to think too highly of himself" and gave way to pride and self-will.

Because of his anger at being deprived of his former habitation because he had sinned, Satan came in wrath to man, perhaps with envy at their happiness, and concealed himself in the serpent. By this manner he was able to deceive Eve and bring about the fall of man.[10] Their sin resulted in all the evils that attend disobedience and Wesley calls such sin and its fruits the "works of the devil." Christ is pictured as being manifested to destroy the "works of the devil" and these works are named as pride, self-will, and love of the world. Also infirmities, weaknesses, pain, and such like, are also works of the devil and, although not destroyed in this life, will be after death.[11]

Is the devil then responsible for man's sin? Wesley will not make man innocent of his crime because of the part Satan played. Some go so far as to make God responsible for man's sin, but this Wesley will not have. However, Wesley does see Satan as the one planting sin in man's heart.

> When Satan had once transfused his own self-will and pride into the parents of mankind, together with a new species of sin,—love of the world, the loving the creature above the Creator,—all manner of wickedness soon rushed in.

Yet man was free and yielded to sin by his own choice. Satan could not have "transfused" anything into man until man had given himself over to the devil. After they had eaten, then evil of every kind rushed in upon them.[12]

The Nature of the First Sin

Wesley believed that the temptation to sin for Adam was very strong. How strong we do not know and the circumstances of it we do not know. It was this strong "temptation from without" that overcame Adam's inclination to holiness, and he lost the love and image of God by "yielding to the temptation."[13] Wesley does not make temptation in itself to be sin, but the yielding to it.[14]

There have been those who think Wesley shares the views of some that sin is basically sexual desire.[15] However, careful analysis of Wesley does not bear out such a thought. He does indicate that Adam might have been led to eat the fruit after Eve had eaten because of her charm,[16] but he makes the root of the sin to be idolatry. William Law in his *Spirit of Prayer* has a theory of the fall that Wesley rejects.

> God then divided the human nature into a male and female creature: otherwise man would have brought forth his own likeness out of himself: in the same manner as he had a birth from God. But Adam let in an adulterous love of the world: by this his virginity was lost, and he had no longer a power of bringing forth a birth from himself.[17]

To this Wesley answers, "We have no shadow of proof for all this." Law further states, "God took this Eve out of him, as a lesser evil, to avoid a greater. For it was a less folly to love the female part of himself, than to love things lower than himself." To this Wesley answers that such are not the words either of Moses or Christ. It is not folly for Christ to love His church , nor for a man to love his wife.[18]

Dr. Taylor in his *Doctrine of Sin* argued that Adam along with his original righteousness had a sinful propensity that "must be so strong as to overcome his (supposed) inbred propensity to holiness." This "supposed original righteousness was consistent with a sinful propensity, vastly stronger and more malignant than ever was or can be in any of his posterity.'" This "sinful propensity" in Adam along with original righteousness is denied by Wesley. He cannot agree that it was a sinful propensity that overcame holiness but a strong temptation to which he yielded.[19]

It is clear to this point that Adam's sin was not brought on him by any necessity either from without or within. There was the temptation and the subtle tempter; there was the charming wife who had been deceived; there was the power of wrong choice and the possibility of erring. Yet the sin of Adam was a free act of his own and cannot be blamed on anyone else. He was fully accountable.[20]

Wesley sums up the nature of the fall of Adam by pointing out that his sin was unbelief—he chose to believe Satan rather than God. It was pride. Even after he sinned he would not acknowledge his fault, but blamed Eve and Satan, and even blamed God when he said, "The woman whom thou gavest to be with me…" There is no acknowledgement of his fault and no humiliation for his sin. This first sin was revolt and rebellion. Adam chose to do his own will rather than the Creator's. He "knowingly and deliberately rebelled against his Father and King."[21] "By this wilful act of disobedience to his Creator, this flat rebellion against his Sovereign, he openly declared that he would no longer have God rule over him; that he would be governed by his own will" and seek his happiness in the world and in his own works.[22] He thus became an idolater—a lover of the world more than lover of God.

The Consequent Loss

Since we have seen the original nature of man and the lovely place into which he was placed before the fall, and since we have seen the terrible sin that he committed, it is now our task to see what Wesley thought man lost when he sinned. Did he lose everything or only a part of his original blessedness?

When Adam sinned, he lost the moral likeness to God. In the day that he ate of the forbidden fruit he died. "The life of God was extinguished in his soul. The glory departed from him. He lost the whole moral image of God, righteousness, and true holiness." He became unholy and unhappy and was full of sin and guilt. His soul was utterly dead to God.[23] He hid himself because he was afraid. His foolish heart was darkened by guilt, sorrow and fear.[24] When he fell, he lost his original righteousness, his title to God's favor, and his communion with God.[25]

Watts, who is quoted favorably by Wesley, makes this first transgression to include all sins. "Every single offense is a virtual breach of all the commands of God." Therefore our first parents in the first sin violated the whole law of God which act made them guilty of unbelief, irreverence, ingratitude, pride and ambition, sensuality, and robbery.

Thus Adam became "dead in sin" having lost the life of God.[26]

There was a marring of the natural image of God in Adam. He lost it "in part."[27] Sufficient of the natural image remains in all men to justify punishing murderers with death. It is difficult to discover what man would have been like, in Wesley's view, had God not immediately offered grace. It is suggested by him that we could have lost our existence through Adam's sin.[28] Since the natural image included understanding, reason, will or affections and liberty, man could not have continued to exist if such had been lost. The understanding was darkened and impaired so that ignorance and mistake take the place of a perfect judgment.[29] Man would still possess an immaterial principle, a spiritual nature, which would have understanding, affections and a degree of liberty. He would have the power of self-motion and self-government, and a natural conscience which likely is a result of grace.[30] Any good connected with these qualities are a result of free grace bestowed on man because of Jesus Christ.[31] This fact will be further explored in the chapter on "Prevenient Grace."

In place of man's likeness to God man now has a likeness to the devil. Because Adam was afraid and wanted to hide from God, and because he was unholy and unhappy and had sunk into pride and self-will, he became the "very image of the devil." Because of sensual appetites and desires he was the image of the beasts that perish. Satan has stamped his own image on the heart of man in self-will. However, man in his idolatry leaves Satan behind because the devil does not love the world. In some ways he is as low as, if not lower than, the goat.[32] Satan holds man captive and blinds, chains, and binds him down.[33]

Sugden in commenting on Wesley's "image of the devil" in man says, "It is utterly wrong to say that we bear the image of the devil."

> Not only was the natural image of God retained; the eternal sense of right and wrong and good and evil was not suffered to be effaced, and thus the elements of the moral image also were shielded from absolute violation… The fall was the utter ruin of nothing in our humanity; only the depravation of every faculty. The human mind retains the principles of truth; the heart the capacity of holy affections; the will its freedom, not yet the freedom of necessary evil.[35]

One must remember, however, that this description of man by Dr.

Pope is understood to be man with the benefits of prevenient grace and not man by nature. In the fall man sank "partly into the image of the devil,—in pride, malice, and all other diabolic tempers,—partly into the image of the brute, being fallen under the dominion of brutal passions and groveling appetites."[36] Wesley also writes that from "the devil the spirit of independence, self-will and pride, productive of all ungodliness and unrighteousness, quickly infused themselves into the hearts of our first parents in paradise."[37]

That Wesley believed in the complete fall of original man there should be no doubt. He makes human nature to be sensual and "devilish" and even fallen lower than the beast.[38] Fletcher, a close friend and companion of Wesley, maintains that Wesley believed in and taught the *"total fall of man in Adam."*[39] The loss for man in the fall was complete and all he now has will be a result of God's free grace, but there will be more of this in a later chapter.

The Threatened Penalty

In his contest with Dr. Taylor, Wesley maintained that Taylor was wrong in making the "death" of Genesis threatened to Adam to be only temporal death. Taylor goes to great length to prove that the death as a penalty for sin was only physical death. He says the passage in Romans 5 "speaks of temporal death, and no other." "He (Paul) evidently speaks of that death which 'entered into the world' by Adam's sin: that death which is common to all mankind..."[40] H. Shelton Smith says that Taylor believed that "the only kind of death with which he (Adam) was threatened was physical, not moral. If he disobeyed, he would be reduced to dust."[41]

Wesley will admit that Paul is speaking of temporal death in Romans 5:12-19, but he denies that it is temporal only.[42] To make it temporal only is to make God a liar because Adam did not die physically in the day he ate. But he did die a spiritual death.[43] "It remains that the death expressed in the original threatening, and implied in the sentence pronounced upon man, includes all evils which could befall his soul and body; death temporal, spiritual, and eternal."[44]

Wesley quotes Dr. Watts to further answer Dr. Taylor:

> But Dr. Taylor is sure, only temporal death was to be the consequence of his disobedience. "For death is the loss of life, and must be understood according to the nature of the life to which it is opposed." Most true; and the life to which it is here opposed, the life Adam enjoyed, till lost by sin, was not only bodily life, but that principle of holiness which the Scripture terms *the life of God.* It was also a title to eternal life. All this, therefore, he lost by sin. And that justly; for death is the" due "wages of sin," death, both temporal, spiritual, and eternal.[45]

For Wesley, Adam and Eve died the moment they partook of the fruit. "The life of God was extinguished in the soul." The soul was utterly dead to God. In this condition he would have entered eternal death had he died physically. His body did begin to die by becoming "obnoxious to weakness, sickness and pain."[46] Thus we can conclude that the threatened penalty included immediate spiritual death and the immediate beginning of physical death which would culminate in eternal death except for God's free grace.

The Curse

Not only is there the threatened penalty of death on man, but the fall brings a curse upon man that affects his whole environment. The body becomes mortal and it presses down the soul. It often hinders the soul and serves it very imperfectly. Man is subject to a thousand mistakes and will continue to be while connected with flesh and blood.[47] Woman in pain will bring forth children and shall be inferior to man. Man shall work amongst thorns and thistles and pain and labor shall be his lot. The very nature of the body after the fall is such that the "seeds of death are sown in our very nature." Thus into man's own body is placed a curse that brings misery, sorrow and pain.[48]

The rest of God's creation is also affected by this curse. The ground is cursed and brings forth thorns and thistles. No longer can man dwell in the Garden of Eden. Violent winters, sultry summers and solar heat are all a result of the fall.[49] Earthquakes are God's strange works of judgment sent to punish because of sin.[50] For Wesley all the things that harm or destroy in the earth come because of the fall of man.

All the fierceness among animals comes as a result of the fall.

They are deprived of their perfections. They harm each other and they harm man. Even the lack of beauty in them is a part of the curse. They even now suffer from the brutality of man whom they were to serve and obey. Man's sin has brought untold misery to the animal kingdom.[51] By his sin Adam "entitled all his posterity to error, guilt, sorrow, fear, pain, diseases, and death."[52]

Endnotes

1. *Works*, II, 31.
2. *Ibid.*, 31.
3. Cannon, *op. cit.*, 195.
4. *Works*, II, 70.
5. *Ibid.*, 31-32.
6. *Ibid.*, 70.
7. *Ibid.*, 32.
8. *Ibid.*, 405.
9. *Ibid.*, 531.
10. *Ibid.*, 70.
11. *Ibid.*, 71-73.
12. *Ibid.*, 473-474.
13. *Ibid.*, V, 597.
14. *Ibid.*, VI, 515.
15. Lipsky, *op. cit.*, 120. Lee, *op. cit.*, 75.
16. *Works*, II, 32.
17. *Ibid.*, V, 676.
18. *Ibid.*, 676.
19. *Ibid.*, 597. see also John Taylor, *The Scripture-Doctrine of Original Sin*, Belfast: John Hay, Bookseller, 1746, 166.
20. *Ibid.*, II, 39.
21. *Ibid.*, 33-36.
22. *Ibid.*, I, 400.
23. *Ibid.*, II, 71.
24. *Ibid.*, 32.
25. *Ibid.*, V, 631-632.
26. *Ibid.*, 640-641.
27. *Ibid.*, II, 36.

28. *Ibid.*, 554-560.
29. *Ibid.*, II, 36.
30. *Ibid.*, II, 479.
31. *Ibid.*, I, 482.
32. *Ibid.*, 396-401.
33. *Ibid.*, 339.
34. Sugden, *op. cit.*, II, 219-220. See Pope, *op. cit.*, II, 58.
35 Pope, *op. cit.*, II, 58.
36. *Works,* II, 42.
37. *Ibid.*, 474.
38. *Ibid.*, 478.
39. John Fletcher, *Works*, New York: B. Waugh and T. Mason, 1835, I, 12-16 (Now available from Schmul Publishing Co., Nicholasville, KY).
40. John Taylor, *op. cit.*, 28.
41. H. Shelton Smith, *Changing Conceptions of Original Sin*, New York: Charles Scribner's Sons, 1955, 15.
42. *Works*, V, 529
43. *Ibid.*, I, 401.
44. *Ibid.*, V, 528.
45. *Ibid.*, 641.
46. *Ibid.*, II, 71.
47. *Works*, II, 34.
48. *Ibid.*, 33-35.
49. *Ibid.*, 27.
50. *Ibid.*, I, 507.
51. *Ibid.*, II, 53-54.
52. *Ibid.*, 36.

Chapter 4

The Universality of Sin

To this point we have observed first Wesley's view of original man in his created bliss and holiness and then his view of man in his disobedience with its resulting loss to man. None of this could have been known except by revelation. Wesley was also a close observer of mankind in general, both in history and in his contemporaries. Were not all men sinful? He believed so and proved it both by Scripture and by observation. He was not only interested in the fact that they were all evil but also wanted to know why. One could establish the first fact—the universality of sin—by observation, although the Bible also bears witness to it. The finding of the answer to the question why men are sinful required a special revelation.[1]

In his *Doctrine of Original Sin* Wesley answers Dr. Taylor by discussing both the fact of man's sinful state and the reason for it. He says the fact must first be established before the attempt to account for it be made. So he first inquires "what is the real state of mankind" and endeavors "to account for it."[2] We shall follow this same plan. In this chapter there will be an investigation of the universality of sin; in the next chapter the transmission of sin will be considered.

Wesley's View Before Georgia

In 1735, at the age of thirty-two, Wesley went to Georgia as a missionary to the Indians. What was his attitude at this time toward human nature? There was much idealization of the Indians and other primitives in the Eighteenth Century. The Indians were supposed to have escaped the corruptions of civilization and to have retained an original simplicity.[3] Cannon believes Wesley went to Georgia with a high view of the Indian as the "noble savage" of Rousseau's philosophy.

He quotes Wesley from a letter written to Dr. John Burton on October 10, 1735, just four days before sailing.[4]

> I hope to learn the true sense of the gospel of Christ by preaching it to the heathen. They have no comments to construe away the text: no vain philosophy to corrupt it; no luxurious, sensual, covetous, ambitious expounders to soften its unpleasing truths, to reconcile earthly-mindedness and faith, the Spirit of Christ and the spirit of the world. They have no party, no interest to serve, and are therefore fit to receive the gospel in simplicity. They are as little children, humble, willing to learn, and eager to do the will of God.[5]

Years later Wesley states that by hearsay he had understood the Indians to have "Temperance, Justice, and Veracity."[6] In his sermon on "Original Sin," which was written at the time of his controversy with Dr. Taylor, he refers to those "fair pictures of human nature which men have drawn in all ages." These men have given "gay descriptions of the dignity of man" and tried to show the "fair side of human nature." By this time in his life, however, Wesley is far from agreeing.[7]

In his sermon on "The Circumcision of the Heart" written in January of 1733, two years before his going to Georgia, Wesley is convinced that man in his best estate is "all sin and vanity." He claims that the "unreasonable, earthly, sensual, devilish passions usurp authority over our will; in a word, that there is no whole part in our soul, that all the foundations of our nature are out of course."[8] During these same years Wesley was seeking holiness and believed that his endeavors to the utmost of his ability to keep the whole law were accepted of God.[9] Although Wesley believed in the corruption of men's nature by sin when he went to Georgia, he did not seem to be sure at that time that all men are so corrupted.

The Observation of the Indians

Upon his arrival in America Wesley had the opportunity to see the heathen with his own eyes. Although he was not privileged to give his time to their conversion, he did contact them sufficiently to give a vivid description of them. Some had no religion at all. Each did what was right in his own eyes and had two short rules—to do what he will, and what he can. They are all, except the Choctaws, "gluttons, drunkards, thieves, dissemblers, liars." They murder fathers, mothers and children. It is not uncommon for a son to shoot his father or mother because they are old and past labor. Mothers will destroy an unwanted child; a father will leave his wife at his own pleasure, cut the throats of her children by him and go his way. A young Indian woman seldom refuses anyone.[10]

Speaking of the Creek Indians Wesley writes that nothing will restrain them from drunkenness and other European vices. They are "exquisite dissemblers" and they know not what friendship or gratitude is. "They show no inclination to learn anything, but least of all, Christianity, being fully as opinionated of their own parts and wisdom, as either modern Chinese or ancient Romans."[11] Comparing the Indians of the north and south in America Wesley says the northern ones are idolaters of the worst kind while the ones in the south have no religion at all. The Chickasaws, who seem to have some idea of a supreme being, are depraved by what they think their god tells them.[12]

Thus Wesley's observations of the Indians did not confirm any notion of the dignity of man.

> Suffice it to say that when Wesley left Georgia he entertained quite a different concept of the noble savage. He had seen him in his own haunts and observed his behavior and his character. For the first time in his life, Wesley began to understand empirically the meaning of original sin.[13]

He did see in the Indians, however, some things better than he could see in some Christians. In referring to a group of so-called Christians in England, he remarked that they "were indeed more savage in their behavior than the wildest Indians I have yet met with."[14] On another occasion he admired the reverence the Indians showed their deity compared to that shown by many Christians.[15] However, following his contacts with the heathen Wesley sees something deep down in all men that makes for universal corruption.

The Influence of His Conversion Experience

Wesley returned from Georgia in 1738 a disillusioned man, not only to the condition of human nature as found in the Indians, but also to his own condition. He had been an earnest seeker for perfection, or heart holiness, for a number of years. It had been somewhat of a vain search, but he continued it with increasing energy.[16] He lists as one of his reasons for going to America to be the "hope of saving my own soul."[17] During the time in America he felt that he was beating the air.[18] His own works and efforts were not gaining him the salvation he sought. On his return to England in January, 1738, he wrote,

> By the most infallible proofs, inward feeling, I am convinced,
> 1. Of unbelief; having no such faith in Christ as will prevent my heart from being troubled;...
> 2. Of pride; throughout my life past; inasmuch as I thought I had what I find I have not:
> 3. Of gross recollection; inasmuch as in a storm I cry to God every moment; in a calm, not;
> 4. Of levity and luxuriance of spirit; recurring whenever the pressure is taken off...[19]

The place of the Moravians in helping to bring Wesley to his true faith in Christ and an account of his conversion have already been given in this book. His heart-warming experience on May 24, 1738, changed his outlook on life and clarified his thinking. He could now see the utter helplessness of man and the need for a victory of faith in Christ. To enter the Kingdom of God one must see his utterly lost condition and what he is by nature. Salvation is not for the good who attain it, but for the bad who need it.[20]

After his conversion, Wesley could see the depth of sin in every man as the real condition that needed salvation. Less than a month after his conversion Wesley preached,

> Wherewithal then shall a sinful man atone for any the least of his sins? With his own Works. No. Were they ever so many or holy, they are not his own, but God's. But indeed they are all unholy and sinful themselves, so that everyone of them needs a fresh atonement. Only corrupt fruit grows on a corrupt tree. And his heart is altogether corrupt and abominable... Therefore having nothing, neither righteousness nor good works to plead, his mouth is utterly stopped before God.[21]

Cannon ably says, "His voyage to America, his ministry in Georgia, and his contact with the redskins proved beyond doubt the inadequacy of the doctrines he held."[22] When he sees justification by faith alone and enters into an experience of that faith, his concept of the complete corruption of human nature deepens.

The Conflict with John Taylor

Considerable reference has already been made to Wesley's argument with Taylor over original sin. Taylor's special work on that subject had been scattered throughout England and Wesley met it wherever he went.[23] Taylor recognizes that there is great wickedness in the earth,[24] but denies the possibility of a just estimate of it. He thinks we can censure the heathen too much. Even if men are universally wicked, this does not prove they are naturally inclined to evil.[25]

Taylor believed it was "highly injurious to the God of our nature, whose hands have formed and fashioned us, to believe our nature is originally corrupted." And he adds, "To disparage our nature is to disparage the work and gifts of God." He felt that to make our nature worse than brutes is to make man act worse than brutes. Such a theory makes men into infidels.[26] He also taught that the earth was not much different today than when God made it.[27] Wesley asks,

> Is it any wonder, that these accounts are very readily received by the generality of men? For who is not easily persuaded to think favorably of himself? Accordingly, writers of this kind are most universally read, admired and applauded. And innumerable are the converts they have made, not only in the frivolous, but in the learned world. So that it is now quite unfashionable to talk otherwise, to say anything to the disparagement of human nature; which is generally allowed, notwithstanding a few infirmities, to be very innocent, and wise, and virtuous![28]

There were some men in England who wrote answers to Taylor's attack on original sin before Wesley wrote his. Wesley quotes extracts from the writings of Dr. Watts, Mr. Hebden, Mr. Boston, and Dr. Jennings. Taylor's work had a great influence in America and drew forth an "unusually penetrating polemic" by Jonathan Edwards.[29] Although Taylor deals mostly with the facts of the transmission of sin, which subject will be dealt with in the next chapter, Wesley feels that Taylor lays himself open to the charge of making man good by nature. Wesley is so convinced that man is universally evil and corrupted that he proceeds to show it in various ways.

Conditions Before the Flood

Here Wesley goes to the Scriptural account to prove the complete degeneracy of man at the time of the flood. He bases his opinion on the account in Genesis 6 where God "saw that the wickedness of man was great, and that every imagination of the thoughts of his heart was only evil continually." God saw that "all flesh had corrupted his way upon the earth," and "the earth is filled with violence through them." Men according to Wesley had been corrupting themselves for sixteen hundred years, and they were all ripe for destruction except Noah and his family.[30]

This group before the flood was the whole human race. No doubt the world was in a much better condition than now as far as beauty, fruitfulness, and seasons were concerned. Men lived to a great age and likely were very numerous in the earth. The universal destruction of men proved their universal corruption.[31]

Wesley sees that these men were evil within—the soul, the inward man, his "inclination, affection, passion, appetite, every temper, design and thought." The whole thereof was "evil;—contrary to moral rectitude, contrary to the nature of God," contrary to all that God had seen to be good when he created man. Wesley cannot find any good mixed with the evil. There were some motions placed into their hearts by God urging repentance, but still "in his flesh dwelt no good thing." All his nature was evil unmixed with good. Apart from any grace that God might give him this man at the time of the flood was evil continually; there was no deviation into the good.[32]

Nature of Heathen Life

Wesley brings forth Scriptural evidence to show that man became corrupted again after the flood.[33] Then he goes into secular history to see what the heathen world was like. One need go no farther than the Romans who were "full of envy, murder, debate, deceit, malignity; whisperers, backbiters, despiteful, proud, boasters, disobedient to parents, covenant breakers, without natural affection, implacable, unmerciful."[34]

Wesley sees many heathen as of the basest sort inferior to the beasts. They kill, are savage even more than lions who only kill what they need for food. He cannot see any dignity of human nature there![35] They are without God in the world; they either do not know Him at all, or else have ideas that are worse than none. They have no social virtues and have no regard for truth or justice.

> Such are the moral, such the intellectual perfections, according to the latest and most accurate accounts, of the present heathens, who are diffused in great numbers over a fourth part of the known world.[36]

Wesley examines the people of Asia. He finds many reports make them to be the glory of mankind and a pattern for all Europe. But Wesley cannot believe these reports. He finds these people to be lazy and proud, dishonest and robbers. Nor do they have a proper concept of God. They worship Confucius and their ancestors. The heathen of Muscovy and Sweden are no better. They are savage; they are idolaters of the basest and vilest kind. So again Wesley concludes, "Thus have we seen what is the present state of the heathens in every part of the known world; and these still make up, according to the previous calculation, very near two-thirds of mankind."[37]

Nature of More Civilized Man

Wesley continues by an examination of the Mohammedans. He finds their Koran contains the most gross and impious absurdities. One can see they do not love or know God, not only because of their horrible notions about him, but also because they do not love their brothers. They are cruel murderers and are destroyers of mankind.[38] They are utter strangers to all true religion as are their "four-footed brethren." They are as void of mercy as lions and tigers and are given to lusts as are bulls and goats. They are a disgrace to human nature. He believes they are but little, if any, better than the heathen around them.[39]

What about the Christian part of the world? The Christians are little better than the Turks when they live in the Turkish dominions. Even those in many other places do not appear to be much better. Those who live in the western world seem to have the advantage. They have more knowledge and better forms of worship. Yet two-thirds are in the Church of Rome and most of them are entirely unacquainted with either the theory or practice of religion.[40] When persecution ended for the church and honor came to the Christian profession, the Christians rushed headlong into all kinds of vices. From the time of Constantine to the Reformation Satan ruled, and the church was in a deplorable state.

Have things been better since the Reformation? Wesley fears not. People were reformed in their opinions and in modes of worship, but there was failure in reforming tempers and lives. Even their own leaders despaired of their accomplishments. Are any of these reformed Christians better than heathen nations? In justice, mercy and truth Wesley thinks not. Although there are Christian individuals in many nations, "yet the whole world never did, nor can at this day, show a Christian country or city."[41]

Another undeniable proof for Wesley that the world is out of course is the fact that there is war. He says it cannot be reconciled to religion, reason or sense. When men make war their last resort what further proof need we of the utter degeneracy of all nations! And yet we talk of the dignity of our present nature![42]

The Complete Corruption of Man

Wesley says, "Look out of your doors," and you can see the vices of men.[43] The Scriptures declare man to be full of "wounds, and bruises, and putrefying sores." And the daily experience of man confirms this account. By nature man has no knowledge, no love, no fear of God. He is an atheist and a rank idolater. He possesses the image of the devil, is as the beasts and loves the world.[44]

Sugden says that Wesley exaggerates the picture of universal sin. "What he does try to convey is that anterior to, and apart from, the revelation of God's pardoning love in Jesus Christ, man is absolutely and hopelessly under the control of evil, and this is not true."[45] But

Wesley believed that by nature one is wholly corrupted, and by grace would be wholly renewed. He felt strongly that this doctrine of the total corruption of man was the basic difference between heathenism and Christianity.

> But here is the *shibboleth:* Is man by nature filled with all manner of evil? Is he void of all good? Is he wholly fallen? Is his soul totally corrupted? Or, to come back to the text, is "every imagination of the thoughts of his heart evil continually?" Allow this, and you are so far a Christian. Deny it, and you are but a heathen still.[46]

Reasons for the Corruption

Why is man so universally corrupted? It cannot be explained by example or custom. It is true that men follow one another, but how account for the custom? Why is custom all on the side of vice rather than virtue? Some answer that education is bad and accounts for the bad ways of men. Wesley admits education is strong, and that in most cases it is bad. But this is not the solution. How am I to account of the almost universal prevalence of bad education? Wesley wants to know when and how it came to prevail. The very first sinners could not have had a bad education. Wickedness must have come first.[47]

Nor will the fact of the power to choose wrong in each individual account for every man's sinning. It can account for Adam, and maybe for one-half the human race, but Wesley cannot see that it could account for the total corruption of man. "I cannot possibly, on this supposition, account for the general wickedness of mankind in all ages and nations." He feels we must look deeper to find the cause of the universality of sin than in custom, education, or the native power of choice.[48]

Wesley of course believes that man was originally corrupted as was pointed out in the last chapter. All men share in this corruption because Adam sinned as shall be pointed out in the next chapter. It is impossible for Wesley to believe that man was always as he is now.

> If I believed this,—that men were originally what they are now,—if you could once convince me of this, I could not go so far as to be a Deist.

> I must either be a Manichee or an Atheist. I must either believe there was an evil God, or that there was no God at all.[49]

For Wesley the only true and rational way of accounting for the general wickedness of mankind everywhere is to be found in the fact that in Adam all die.[50]

Endnotes

1. *Works*, V, 524.
2. *Ibid.*, 493.
3. Lee, *op. cit.*, 70.
4. Cannon, *op. cit.*, 71-72.
5. Original not available for examination. Cited in Cannon, *op. cit.*, 72.
6. *Works*, V, 11.
7. *Ibid.*, I, 392.
8. *Ibid.*, 148.
9. *Works*, III, 71.
10. *Ibid.*, 49.
11. *Ibid.*, 50.
12. *Works*, V, 504-505.
13. Cannon, *op. cit.*, 72.
14. *Works*, III, 60.
15. *Ibid.*, V, 107.
16. *Ibid.*, III, 71-72.
17. Lee, *op. cit.*, 70.
18. *Works*, III, 72.
19. *Ibid.*, 53.
20. *Ibid.*, I, 64.
21. *Ibid.*, 13.
22. Cannon, *op. cit.*, 73.
23. *Works,* V, 492.
24. John Taylor, *op. cit.*, 122.
25. *Ibid.*, 328-329.
26. *Ibid.*, 256-259.
27. *Ibid.*, 318.
28. *Works*, I, 392.
29. Smith, *op. cit.*, 27.

30. *Works*, V, 494.

31. *Works*, I, 393.

32. *Ibid.*, 393-394.

33. *Ibid.*, V, 494.

34. *Ibid.*, I, 339.

35. *Ibid.*, II, 75.

36. *Works*, V, 503.

37. *Ibid.*, 506-507.

38. *Ibid.*, 507-508.

39. *Ibid.*, II, 75.

40. *Ibid.*, 75.

41. *Ibid.*, 63-65.

42. *Ibid.*, V, 511-512.

43. *Works*, V, 522.

44. *Ibid.*, I, 394-397.

45. Sugden, *op. cit.*, II, 209.

46. *Works*, I, 398.

47. *Ibid.*, V, 523-524.

48. *Ibid.*, 566. See Prince, *op. cit.*, 72.

49. *Ibid.*, 574.

50. *Ibid.*, 536.

Chapter 5

The Transmission of Sin

THUS FAR WE HAVE examined Wesley's view of man's original righteousness in a primitive state, and of his disobedience and fall into sin from his holiness and happiness. Also it was seen that Wesley believed that all mankind from that time to the present have been wicked without exception. The question before us now is, "What is the connection between Adam's sin, and the general wickedness of mankind?" Are men now sinful for the same reason that Adam sinned, or is there a sense in which Adam's sin resulted in the corruption of the race?

Taylor's Explanation

We have referred to the controversy between Dr. John Taylor and Wesley. Since Taylor's objections to the orthodox position on original sin were largely at the point of the discussion in this chapter, it is well to analyze his opinions more fully. He was a Presbyterian minister at Norwich. He was an able man and a recognized scholar. Wesley in a letter to him recognized him as a "person of uncommon sense and learning."[1] At one place in his treatise on *Original Sin,* Wesley refers sarcastically to Taylor as a "sweet-tongued orator" who had arisen "not only more enlightened than silly Adam, but than any of his wise posterity."[2] However in most cases Wesley faces Taylor squarely and endeavors to answer all his arguments.

Taylor professes to follow the Scriptures. "I have made the Revelation of God alone the rule of my judgment, not any schemes or opinions of men."[3] In his treatise he wants to know, "How far we, the posterity of Adam, are involved in the consequences of his first transgression." He finds only five passages in the Bible that at all deal with this subject, three times in the New Testament (Romans 5:12-20, I Corinthians 15:21-22, I Timothy 2:14), and twice in the Old Testament (Genesis 2:17, 3:7-11).[4] One can summarize his opinions in the following manner: Adam's sin was personal, and he alone was responsible for it. The death threatened could have been only physical death. There is not too much difference in Adam's nature and that of his posterity. The only way that Adam's posterity sinned in him is that they suffer.

Taylor claims that there is no evidence that Adam's sin is anything but personal. Adam and Eve alone committed the sinful act of disobedience. They were the only ones in the world. He says that in the eye of justice and equity, they alone could be guilty of this deed and therefore blameable and punishable for it.[5] He claims that the death threatened could have been only physical death.

> Death is the losing of life. Death is opposed to life; and must be understood according to the nature of that life to which it is opposed. Now the death here threatened can, with any certainty, be opposed to the life God gave Adam when he created him, verse 7. Anything besides this must be pure conjecture, without a solid foundation.[6]

Taylor does admit widespread corruption in man, but denies it is because of any fault in man's nature.[7] Man's present nature is not too different from that given to Adam and is the work and gift of God.[8] Man's moral abilities and mental powers seem to be about the same as were Adam's.[9]

Taylor finds the passage in Romans 5 the most difficult to handle, but here he can see only physical death, and this death passed upon man, not for their own sins, but for Adam's one sin.

> Death therefore must be understood to have passed upon all mankind, not for that they all have sinned really, properly, and personally. But they have sinned, are made sinners. are subjected to death, through the one offense of one man, that is, of Adam.[10]

In another place he states that men "surely can be sinners in no other sense but as they are sufferers."[11] Thus Taylor sees the only involvement of the race in Adam's sin is that they suffer physically for it.

Watson observes that Dr. Whitby, Taylor, and others, who were sometimes called Arminians, were semi-Pelagian. According to this teaching the posterity of Adam do suffer physical ills because of Adam's sin, and are deprived of physical life, but they do not inherit a sinful nature. He claims that this teaching is not Arminian. Wesley is the true Arminian. It would be wrong to call Taylor a Pelagian, for Pelagianism, as modern Socinianism, teaches that Adam was not impaired by the fall, nor was there any hurt to his posterity.[12] Watson asserts that in his day "most modern writers who deny the doctrine of original sin have followed" Taylor.[13]

Wesley of course found Taylor to be basically wrong. It is in his answer to Taylor that we find Wesley's view on the transmission of sin most clearly defended. We shall now proceed to summarize his view on the connection between Adam and his posterity.

The Headship of Adam

Wesley sees that the grand cause of the universal wickedness of mankind is that "all die in Adam."[14] He believed that Adam was in some sense federal head or representative of all mankind.

> My reason for believing he was so, in some sense, is this: Christ was the representative of mankind, when God "laid on him the iniquities of us all, and he was wounded for our transgressions." But Adam was a type or figure of Christ; therefore, he was also, in some sense, our representative.[15]

He looks upon Adam as representing Adam's posterity as "one collective body."[16]

Wesley is aware that "representative, or federal head, are not Scripture words: it is not worthwhile to contend for them." He thinks the idea is there because that the "state of all mankind did so far depend on Adam, that, by his fall, they all fell into sorrow, and pain, and death, spiritual and temporal." Adam was on trial for all mankind. He as a single person was on trial for himself and for all of us. This does not mean that his posterity could not also be placed on trial for themselves.[17]

This position of Adam as head of the race was effective only for the one act. The condemnation came by "one offense" only. It was not Adam's sins, but "Adam's sin."[18] All men participated in this one sin in some sense. Taylor denied this and claimed that, if they did, it was the "offense of millions" rather than of one. Wesley admits that in one sense it was the offense of one; in another sense, the offense of millions. For all were in Adam since God made of one blood all men. He quotes approvingly that "Adam was a public person, including all his posterity, and, consequently, that all mankind, descending from him by ordinary generation, sinned in him, and fell with him in his first transgression."[19]

The Imputed Guilt

Since mankind sinned in Adam, in what sense then are they guilty? Wesley could not agree with Taylor that men were considered sinners only in the sense that they suffer physically. For him the suffering is a penalty and they could not be punished had they not sinned in some sense.[20] Thus children cannot be looked upon as innocent but "as involved in the guilt of Adam's sin."[21] Taylor, in commenting on verse 12 in Romans 5— "Death passed upon all men, for that all have sinned"— makes the sinning to be the suffering, and that suffering is the being subjected to death. So Wesley tells Taylor that he makes the apostle to say, "All are subjected to death, because all are subjected to death."[22] But Wesley believes all are subject to death because all have sinned in Adam.

Wesley would agree with this following summary of Augustine's position:

> All were one in his nature by virtue of that power through which he could procreate. Since they are out of him they were in him, since he included the universal nature of man within himself, the fall has been a universal one… One can perhaps call original sin a strange sin in that it was committed not by us, but by Adam. It is at the same time our own sin since we were in him in a certain sense and have inherited it from him.[23]

Although Wesley believes that children can be involved in the guilt of parents' sins, he believes there is a "sound and Scriptural" distinction between personal sin and imputed guilt.[24] Watson describes two kinds of imputations—mediate and immediate. The immediate is the accounting of Adam's sin to be ours as if we were one moral person with him. This is false. Mediate imputation is the suffering of mortality and corruption of moral nature because of Adam's sin. He says this is not enough. Then he quotes from Watts who is also quoted by Wesley as giving the better view.

> But it may be asked, "How can the acts of the parent's treason be imputed to his little child, since those acts were quite out of the reach of an infant, nor was it possible for him to commit them?"
>
> Or, "How can the eminent service performed by a father be imputed to his child, who is but an infant?"
>
> I answer: 1. Those acts of treason, or acts of service, are, by a common figure, said to be imputed to the children, when they suffer or enjoy the consequences of their father's treason or eminent service, though the particular actions of treason or service could not be practiced by the children. This would be easily understood, should it occur in human history: and why not, when it occurs in sacred writings.
>
> I answer: 2. Sin is taken either for an act of disobedience to a law, or for the legal result of such an act; that is, the guilt, or liableness to punishment. Now, when we say, the sin of a traitor is imputed to his children, we do not mean, that the act of the father is charged upon the child; but that the guilt, or liableness to punishment, is so transferred to him; that he suffers banishment or poverty on account of it.[25]

Wesley recognized two kinds of guilt—guilt that is personal and accounted to the person who did the act, and guilt in the sense of liability to punishment which may be imputed to another. Dr. Pope says it this way, "The guilt of the first transgression is reckoned in its consequences upon all the race represented by the first transgressor."[26] Thus men "were so constituted sinners by Adam's sinning, as to become liable to the punishment threatened to his transgression."[27] In this manner mankind sinned with Adam.

The Punishment for Original Sin

That Adam was punished for his act in taking the forbidden fruit has already been noticed. May we look upon the miseries and depravation of the human race as punishment for the first sin? It is at this point that Taylor and Wesley differed sharply. While Taylor saw the physical miseries of the human race as natural consequences for the sin of Adam, Wesley saw them as penal consequences. Wesley defined the suffering which results from sin as punishment. The name punishment belongs properly to the sufferings that are inflicted on account of sin, so consequently "it is an evident truth, that the whole animate creation is punished for Adam's sin."[28]

Thus Wesley looked upon all natural evil as punishment for Adam's sin. Nature's disasters are true punishments. The beasts, as well as human beings, suffer this punishment.[29] These evils are the several branches of the curse that befell man in the original fall and extends to all of mankind.[30] The fall brought sin and misery upon the entire human race.[31]

Although Taylor insisted that the death to man for Adam's fall was only physical, Wesley believed it included spiritual and eternal death. This spiritual death was passed on to every child of Adam and includes deep corruption of his nature. Uneasy and unruly passions are coeval with one's understanding and memory. Wesley did not believe that anyone would be punished eternally for Adam's sin, yet the being "dead in sin" would so result, if persisted in.[32]

While Taylor wanted to look upon all human suffering, including death, as a benefit to mankind, Wesley, though admitting that values could come from some of them, saw them as punishments still.[33] The punishments may be mixed with mercy, but they are punishments just the same.[34] For Wesley it seemed strange that, if death were a benefit to mankind, God would threaten it for disobedience in his people. Then he adds two or three obvious questions.

> (I) Did God propose death as a benefit in the original threatening? (II) Did he represent it as a benefit in the sentence pronounced on Adam: "Dust thou art, and unto dust thou shalt return?" (III) Do the inspired writers speak of God's "bringing a flood on the world of the ungodly, as a benefit, or a punishment?" (IV) Do they mention the destruction of Sodom and Gomorrah as designed for a benefit to them? (V) Is it by way of benefit that God declares, "The soul that sinneth it shall die?" Certainly this point is not defensible. Death is properly not a benefit, but a punishment.[35]

Wesley asks, "Why do infants suffer?" If their sufferings were to cure, what would it cure in them? If one says it is for their parents, Wesley answers that it does not have that effect. Their sufferings, as well as those of all mankind, are not from mere mercy, but from justice also. "In other words, they have in them the nature of punishments, even on us and on our children. Therefore children are not innocent before God. They suffer; therefore, they deserve to suffer."[36] Wesley could not logically see how anyone could be punished by God and not deserve it.

Nor could Wesley have regarded anyone innocent by nature. If an infant were not deserving of punishment, why would he need the blood of Christ? And if one were naturally innocent, he would have a natural power to remain so, and thus could avoid ever needing the grace of God in his life.[37]

The State of Infants

It seems that the doctrine of original sin has suffered most when men have considered the state of infants in the scheme. Taylor was unable to see why God would consider children as vile creatures and corrupted in nature and deserving of God's wrath.[38] But Wesley sees the principles of iniquity and sin in children before they can make a moral choice. Even malice, spite, envy and rage are found in their hearts before they can speak. Even though they may be "imitable" in some instances, yet they possess all these evil tempers. "It appears that they are strongly inclined to evil, long before any ill habits can be contracted."[39]

Are infants sinners? Wesley quotes Mr. Hebden to prove so.

> Since Adam's posterity are born liable to death, which is the due "wages of sin," it follows, that they are born sinners. No art can set aside the consequence.
>
> Either Christ is the Savior of infants, or he is not; if he is not, how is he "the Savior of all men?" But, if he is, then infants are sinners: for he suffered death for sinners only. He "came to seek and save" only "that which was lost;" to "save his people from their sins." It follows, that infants are sinners, that they are lost, and, without Christ, are undone forever.[40]

Yet Wesley would not have it that infants who die before reaching the age of choice were lost. He could not hold with the Calvinist that men could be sent to Hell for Adam's sin only.[41] Had there never been grace there could never have been a race for the race would have literally died in Adam without any propagation.[42] Yet by nature every child is under the displeasure of God as is proved by those sufferings that come upon them.[43] Wesley's conclusion on the position of infants could well be summed up in the words of Watson.

> The seeds of the vices which exist in society may be discovered in children in their earliest years; selfishness, envy, pride, resentment, deceit, lying, and often cruelty; and so much is this the case, so explicitly is this acknowledged by all, that it is the principle object of the moral branch of education to restrain and correct these evils...[44]

Natural Generation

This condition of depravity in man, and all the evils attendant therewith, are passed on from one generation to another by natural procreation. God made Adam in his own image, but after the fall Adam could only beget a child in his own likeness which was now depraved. Wesley professes that he does not know how such is done. He is utterly in the dark as to how God forms the body and soul in the womb. But he knows it is done. He will not believe that the bringing forth of a sinful creature makes God chargeable with creating evil. He knows that it is by the power of God that man can produce offspring, but it is not God's fault that that offspring is sinful.[45]

Taylor suggested that the conveying a sinful nature to a child made the act of procreation sinful. But Wesley denies the consequence. "You may transmit to your children a nature tainted with sin, and yet commit no sin in so doing."[46] But, says Taylor, "It is highly dishonorable to God, to suppose he is displeased at us for what he himself has infused into our nature." Wesley answers that he does not "infuse sin into our nature, no more than he infuses sin into our actions; though it is his power that produces both our actions and nature."[47]

What is it that is actually passed from parent to child? Fletcher writes,

> Now, according to the invariable laws of Providence, an upright, holy nature can no more proceed from a fallen, sinful one, than gentle lambs can be begotten by fierce tigers, or harmless doves by venomous serpents. Common sense, therefore, and natural philosophy, dictate that our first parents could not communicate the angelic life which they had lost, nor impart to their children a better nature than their own.[48]

Taylor could not see how a nature could be sinful which is neither caused nor consented to by an individual. But Wesley sees that spite, envy and other evil tempers in children are certainly not virtuous, nor morally good, even though not caused by the child. He says it is contrary to the nature of God and therefore sinful.[49] It is right at this point where these two men have their greatest difficulty. Wesley told Taylor that his capital mistake was in thinking a man had to act holy before he was holy; a person could be holy before any choice.[50] Taylor cannot see a person sinful before he acts. Wesley can, and believes such to be a fundamental fact in human life. In fact such a fact of human sinfulness before any capability of action is the only explanation of universal wickedness.[51]

The Justice of God

Wesley had high regard for the proper concept of the justice of God. He could not see it just for God to be considered the author of sin,[52] nor could he accept the Calvinist idea that men could be sent to Hell for Adam's sin.[53] However, Taylor thought it unjust to have man born sinful because of the failure of the first parent and for children to be born under the divine displeasure. While Taylor thinks it relieves the sense of injustice in God to look upon man in a better light, and only as unfortunate by birth, Wesley is unwilling to say it is not black when it is. The condition is there; now, how account for it? For the evil condition to be there and make God responsible for it, as Taylor does, was the worst kind of injustice. Wesley acknowledges the black picture as it is, but places the blame entirely upon man. Since man suffers, he deserves to suffer.

Wesley sees Taylor admitting that the race could have lost its existence through the sin of Adam.[54] And this extinction would have come on the race because of Adam's sin. This being true, then Adam's posterity could inherit nothing but a nature under the divine displeasure. And it would be wrong to charge God with injustice for their receiving such a nature since that was the only kind of a nature Adam could give.

The real question is, how could God justly permit Adam after the fall to bring forth a posterity who would inherit such a nature? It is right at this point where Wesley's unique teaching of prevenient grace appears. Although prevenient grace is the subject of the next chapter, it should be stated here that Wesley believed that free grace offered to all men completely offset any sense of injustice in permitting the race to exist in a corrupt nature.[55] Fletcher discusses this same point quite at length and concludes, "This leaves us not the least shadow of reason to complain of the Divine proceedings respecting us."[56]

The Natural Man

To conclude this chapter it remains for us to summarize what the human creature is like by nature. One must remember that Wesley uses the term *by nature* to describe man as he is by birth apart from the grace of God. By *original nature* Wesley means the nature that was given to Adam before the fall, and which was completely corrupted by the fall. It is difficult to describe fully man as what he is by nature because, as we now see man, he not only inherits Adam's nature, but is also a recipient of God's grace as we shall later see. Wesley's ideas of man's present corrupt nature are largely drawn from the Bible, from observation and from deductions drawn from the premise of a complete fall in Adam.

This present, corrupt nature of man is under the displeasure of God. Man is destitute of the favor of God,[57] and is a child of wrath.[58] His propensities to evil are not pleasing to God.[59] The sufferings of all prove that men are under God's displeasure.[60]

Man is also polluted. His evil works prove that he is evil at heart.[61] He is spiritually dead with no life whatsoever in him that would awaken him to God. There is a complete lack of that original righteousness given to Adam and, because of that lack, he has natural propensities to sin.[62] He is full of defects and is a complete captive to the devil.[63]

> And in Adam all died, all humankind, all the children of men who were then in Adam's loins. The natural consequence of this is, that everyone descended from him comes into the world spiritually dead, dead to God, wholly dead in sin; entirely void of the life of God; void of the image of God, of all that righteousness and holiness wherein Adam was created. Instead of this, every man born into the world now bears the image of the devil, in pride and self will; the image of the beast, in sensual appetites and desires. This then is the foundation of the new birth, the entire corruption of our nature.[64]

The three Methodist theologians—Fletcher, Watson, and Pope—agree with this conclusion. We have already noticed Fletcher's agreement. Pope observes that "the Scripture never disjoins the condemnation from the depravity: the one is always implied in the other, while both are generally connected with the great salvation." He further writes, "All are not only regarded as sinners, but made sinners also through the inheritance of a nature of itself inclined only to evil."[65]

Watson sees this entire corruption of our nature as a "depravation arising from a deprivation" rather than the infusion of evil into the soul. He says the "depravation, the perversion, the defect of our nature is to be traced to our birth, so that in our flesh is no good thing," and it grows out of man's separation from God and the absence of spiritual life. The corruption of man's moral nature is a necessary consequence of that privation.[66]

Wesley did not guard his statements as carefully as Watson, and one can get the impression from him that he looks upon evil in nature as an infused thing. He does describe fallen man as having no knowledge, no love for God, no fear of God, yet man is born with pride, is a "rank idolater," has been stamped with the image of the devil, is by nature a beast, has the love of the world "deeply rooted in our nature," and is "filled with all manner of evil."[67] Yet Wesley did not believe that God corrupted man's nature; "that corruption is not his work."[68] The universal corruption of man's nature was derived from Adam and he comes corrupt into the world.[69] He does say concerning this corruption that "all men, being by nature 'dead in sin,' cannot of themselves resist the devil; and that, consequently, all who will not accept of help from God are 'taken captive by Satan at his will.'"[70] Wesley sees the fall of Adam to be first the loss of the image of God and the life of God, and in its place the coming of pride and self-will.[71]

So with Wesley, as with Watson, man is corrupted, filled with all evil, inclined to all evil and under the wrath of God because he is deprived of that image of God, that holiness and righteousness, that life of God with which Adam was created. Since man is born with a nature completely void of true righteousness, he is necessarily full of evil and inclined to sin continually. But Wesley does not leave man there. He finds that, set against man's complete corruption, is the redeeming work of Christ. Free grace reaches all the way back to Eden, and no man has lost more through the fall than he can recover through Christ. With this we introduce the theme for our next chapter.

Endnotes

1. *Works*, V, 669.
2. *Ibid.*, 560.
3. John Taylor, *op. cit.*, III.
4. *Ibid.*, 4-5.
5. *Ibid.*, 13-14.
6. *Ibid.*, 7.
7. *Ibid.*, 168.
8. *Ibid.*, 110.
9. *Ibid.*, 170-176.
10. *Ibid.*, 51.
11. *Ibid.*, 33-34.
12. Richard Watson., *Theological Institutes*, New York: Carlton and Porter, 1857, II, 44-45.
13. *Ibid.*, 50. See also Turner, *op. cit.*, 209; Cannon., *op. cit.*, 194; Smith, *op. cit.*, 11; where they make Taylor to be essentially Pelagian.
14. *Works*, V, 538.
15. *Ibid.*, 588.
16. *Ibid.*, 603.
17. *Ibid.*, 588-602.

18. *Ibid.*, 533-535.
19. *Ibid.*, 539-540.
20. *Ibid.*, 535-536.
21. *Ibid.*, 577.
22. *Ibid.*, 534.
23. Spalding, *op. cit.*, 26.
24. *Works*, V, 578.
25. *Ibid.*, 627.
26. W. B. Pope, *op. cit.*, II, 48.
27. *Works*, V, 535.
28. *Ibid.*, 577-580.
29. *Ibid.*, 578-581.
30. *Ibid.*, 527.
31. *Ibid.*, 540.
32. *Ibid.*, 577-583.
33. *Ibid.*, 526.
34. *Ibid.*, 584.
35. *Ibid.*, 537.
36. *Ibid.*, 579.
37. Fletcher, *op. cit.*, III, 327.
38. Taylor, *op. cit.*, 262-263.
39. *Works*, V, 585-586.
40. *Ibid.*, 647.
41. *Ibid.*, I, 482.
42. Fletcher, *op. cit.*, II, 231.
43. *Works*, V, 584.
44. Watson, *op. cit.*, II, 65.
45. *Works*, V, 590-591.
46. *Ibid.*, 553.
47. *Ibid.*, 592.
48. Fletcher, *op. cit.*, III, 318.
49. *Works*, V, 592.
50. *Ibid.*, 561.
51. *Ibid.*, 593.
52. *Ibid.*, 591.
53. *Ibid.*, VII, 97.

54. *Ibid.*, V, 540.
55. *Ibid.*, 541, 555, 589.
56. Fletcher, *op. cit.*, III, 321.
57. *Works*, V, 602, 618.
58. *Ibid.*, 642.
59. *Ibid.*, 562.
60. *Ibid.*, 584.
61. *Ibid.*, 545.
62. *Ibid.*, 635.
63. *Ibid.*, 556.
64. *Ibid.*, I, 401.
65. Pope, *op. cit.*, II, 48-55.
66. Watson, *op. cit.*, II, 79.
67. *Works*, I, 394-398.
68. *Ibid.*, V, 574.
69. *Ibid.*, 542-543.
70. *Ibid.*, 556.
71. *Ibid.*, I, 401.

Chapter 6

Prevenient Grace

As has been noticed Wesley saw no injustice on God's part in allowing man to be born sinful, depraved and guilty and under the divine condemnation because at the same time God's grace is bestowed on him. This grace is a supernatural gift of God to every man. It does not come by way of nature. Man is not a recipient of grace through his birth but at his birth. Wesley calls this grace, "preventing grace," and one cannot understand his concept of sin or salvation without an understanding of this grace.

Definition

The term *prevenient* or, as used by Wesley, *preventing grace* means literally the "grace that goes before." It is used in this sense because Wesley saw that in every man there was something prior to any justification that made a man better than he is by nature. Cannon defines this grace as follows.

> If a man is by nature sinful, conceived in iniquity, he is at the same time endued with the quality of what Wesley calls *Preventing Grace.* There is something in him besides the attributes of his own nature. He is endowed with a spark of divinity. God works in him, not in the sense of momentary intervention or sudden, catastrophic possession, but rather in the sense of an abiding presence and a continual indwelling.[1]

This "spark of divinity," although in every man, is not of man but is given by God.

> For allowing that all the souls of men are dead in sin by *nature,* this excuses none, seeing there is no man that is in a state of mere nature; there is no man, unless he has quenched the Spirit, that is wholly void of the grace of God. No man living is entirely destitute of what is

> vulgarly called *natural conscience.* But this is not natural: it is more properly termed, *preventing grace.* Every man has a greater or less measure of this, which waiteth not for the call of man. Everyone has, sooner or later, good desires; although the generality of men stifle them before they can strike deep root, or produce any considerable fruit. Everyone has some measure of that light, some faint glimmering ray, which sooner or later, more or less, enlightens every man that cometh into the world. And everyone, unless he be one of the small number, whose conscience is seared as with a hot iron, feels more or less uneasy when he acts contrary to the light of his own conscience. So that no man sins because he has not grace, but because he does not use the grace which he has.[2]

It is easily seen from this quotation that Wesley did not hold to a grace limited only to those who will be saved. Nor did he believe that God's grace was irresistible. There was a universal remedy for a universal evil.[3] This grace is given to all men, and Wesley's conception of the operation of this grace "is as far removed from the Calvinistic conception as the east is from the west. Saving grace is not particular; it does not rest on the prior principle of election or predestination."[4]

Wesley says that this grace is *"free in all,* and *free for all."* It does not depend upon any merit or good works in man. Any good tempers or desires in man freely flow from this grace and are not the cause of it. This grace freely comes from God, who gave His only son for man. This grace is freely given to all men and is not limited to a select few who have been chosen to be saved.[5] Thus we can see that grace for Wesley was the unmerited favor of God freely given to all men. It can be resisted, or it can lead a man on to salvation, as will be seen.

Prevenient Grace Derived Through the Atonement

Now it would be possible for God to extend grace to humankind apart from an atonement in Jesus Christ. In fact Wesley admits that even creation itself, with all its blessings upon man, comes from God's mere grace and favor. "It was free grace that 'formed man of the dust of the ground, and breathed into him a living soul,' and stamped on that soul the image of God, and 'put all things under his feet.'" In other words man did not merit anything from God in the beginning, and all blessings before the fall were of God's free grace. This grace continues to man after the fall, but does so because of the atonement. Man cannot receive any grace from God by way of his nature, but all grace shown to sinful man comes because Christ died for sinners.[6] It is through Christ that God can freely give us all things.[7]

It is clear in Wesley that all that was lost in Adam can be regained in Christ.[8] What Adam had before he sinned was given by God out of his love and grace. Adam lost it all because he sinned, and so could not have imparted to his posterity anything. In fact Adam would have had no posterity had no redemption been provided. So his very ability to continue in existence, and propagate a race, was dependent upon God's grace which now is bestowed on the basis of the atonement.[9] Wiley says,

> But even the heinousness of his sin and the shame of his fall did not result in the utter destruction of his being. The unseen hand of the promised Redeemer prevented it. Thus the mystery of sin and the mystery of grace met at the gate of Eden.[10]

Benefits to the Race

It can thus be seen that all blessings of mankind are a result of the atonement and of the free grace that flows therefrom. And this grace reaches as far as the human race has gone. These blessings are many and come automatically, although in various degrees, to every member of the race. "They are the fruits of free grace, and not the root. They are not the cause, but the effects of it. Whatsoever good is in man, or is done by man, God is the author and doer of it."[11]

As already noted grace saved the race from extinction. Had the case been closed with Adam's sin, the penalty would have intervened and Adam would have died. As a consequence, "the race would have perished in its root. Under law the race did so perish."[12]

> But for the immediate intervention of a redemptive economy, the penalty of death must have been promptly executed according to its own terms. The execution must have precluded the propagation and existence of the race.[13]

So one can say that the very fact of life itself, and all blessings as a result of life, are a direct result of the grace that has been given to every man.

This prevenient grace removes for every man the guilt inherited from Adam for his sin. Concerning the text, "As by one man's disobedience all were made sinners, so by the obedience of one, all were made righteous," Wesley has this to say: "By the merits of Christ, all men are cleared from the guilt of Adam's actual sin."[14] None will ever die eternally merely for the sin of Adam.[15] All the imputed guilt of original sin is removed in Christ. Man by nature is guilty of Adam's sin, but, through the free gift of grace, the guilt is removed. No one actually exists with the guilt of Adam's sin hanging over his head for it is removed in Christ. This can be called "infant justification" and means that all infants who die before accountability would be saved through Christ. In fact Wesley could see no need of a Savior for children who die if they were not guilty through Adam. It is from that guilt that Christ becomes their Savior.[16]

> As to infants, they are not, indeed, born justified or regenerate; so that to say that original sin is taken away, as to infants by Christ, is not the correct view of the case, for the reasons before given: but they are all born under the "free grace," the effects of the "righteousness" of one, which extended to all men; and this free gift is bestowed on them in order to justification of life, the adjudging of the condemned to live.[17]

Infants are not justified in the sense that they are regenerated and have the life of God in them. They are only justified in the sense that they are not held accountable for Adam's sin. They still bear the guilt of Adam's sin in the sense that they suffer and die, and also in the sense that they are depraved and are under divine displeasure because of that depravity. But they are not left guilty in the sense that they would die eternally for the first sin. In a letter to a friend, Wesley wrote,

> One of Mr. Fletcher's Checks considers at large the Calvinistic supposition, "that a natural man is *as dead as a stone:* and shows the utter falseness and absurdity of it: seeing that no man living is without some preventing grace; and every degree of grace is a degree of life.

> That "by the offence of one, judgment came upon all men" (all born into the world) "unto condemnation," is an undoubted truth, and affects every infant, as well as every adult person. But it is equally true, that, "by the righteousness of one, the free gift came upon all men" (all born into the world, infant or adult) "unto justification." Therefore no infant ever was, or ever will be, "sent to hell for the guilt of Adam's sin;" seeing it is cancelled by the righteousness of Christ, as soon as they are sent into the world.[18]

Not only does prevenient grace save the race from extinction and remove the guilt of Adam's sin, but it also enables man's natural powers. Lee calls it an "empowering" grace.[19] Although man is not born with any innate knowledge of God, yet he has the ability to learn the knowledge of God from his works.[20]

> For God hath also, through the intercession of his Son, given us his Holy Spirit, to renew us both in knowledge, in his natural image:—opening the eyes of our understanding, and enlightening us with all such knowledge as is requisite to our pleasing God.

He even gives us capacities and opportunities for attaining more than if man had not fallen.[21]

Man is so depraved by nature that he cannot even will what is pleasing to God. His power of choosing the right is gone. He cannot perform his duties in this fallen state apart from grace. But the grace of God enables him to do his duty and to choose the right.[22] For Wesley "human freedom and liberty of the moral agent are of tremendous importance." How then can fallen man respond to the calls of God? "Now this grace (preventing) is the source of all active responsiveness and all good desires spring solely from it."[23] Wesley writes,

> Natural free-will, in the present state of mankind, I do not understand: I only assert there is a measure of free-will supernaturally restored to every man, together with that supernatural light which "enlightens every man that cometh into the world."[24]

Wesley gives an important place to reason, but sees that it needs the assisting power of the Holy Spirit. Reason by the Holy Spirit enables one to understand the Scriptures and to comprehend God's methods of dealing with the children of men. By the Spirit's opening the eyes of our understanding the reason enables one to understand the plan of salvation, and to know what God requires.[25]

Another benefit of prevenient grace to the race is that it restores to man his conscience. While many call this faculty "natural conscience," Wesley prefers to call it a "supernatural gift of God, above all his natural endowments." It is the true light, the Son of God, the Spirit, given to man as a check when he goes contrary to that light. It is an inward monitor that excuses or accuses; it is superadded by the grace of God and is found in every child of man in a greater or lesser degree. It causes some desire to please God, and enables one to know what may or may not please.[26]

Benefits to the Individual

By benefiting the race this prevenient grace benefits every individual within the race. In fact it is an advantage to be a part of the race rather than a being completely distinct from all others. This state makes it possible for each man to be redeemed. If he falls, he can rise again. He does inherit from Adam an evil nature and a weak humanity, but he is also a recipient of a grace that can restore when one falls.[27] This is much better than being left on one's own, for then one sin would forever settle an eternal destiny.

> Human nature is lost, and yet we are still *the offspring of God.* The natural and moral image—essentially one in creation—has departed in its glory, and yet it is recognized as in some sense still existing. Every man is born condemned, and yet he is bidden not to put from him life. He is by nature able neither to think nor feel nor act aright; yet he is throughout Scripture appealed to as if his duty were simply matter of his will. In short original sin and original grace met in the mystery of mercy at the very gate of Paradise.[28]

So then every creature in the human family can be redeemed. Even though he is born sinful and has rebelled in his own heart against God, yet this grace draws him toward God. By this grace he can avoid sin. He can do his duty as a moral creature. He has the mercy of Calvary extended to him. It is his duty, privilege, and possibility to be saved.[29]

By this grace man can turn to God and be saved. There is no way that he can do it of himself for in himself there is no merit nor power.[30]

But this grace enables him to repent and believe. Even the heathen are without excuse because they have this light given to them.[31] Thus every individual can be saved if he will.

This grace can be killed in the individual. He can quench the Spirit and fail to cooperate with the God-given grace.

> Man is able, not just to resist the grace of God, but actually to kill the grace of God which is already housed within him. In this sense, therefore, in making himself immune to the promptings of what some call natural conscience, and what others call divine grace, he steels himself against the power of the Gospel, stifles the first urges to repentance, and dulls himself forever to the raptures of faith. In this negative way, man is the absolute master of his fate and the captain of his salvation…
>
> Granting, therefore, man's ability to stifle and to kill the grace of God within him, have we the right to ascribe to him the positive role of a cooperator with God? We have…
>
> Wesleyan thought, therefore, is decidedly synergistic in its description of the operations prior to justification and essential to the bestowal of saving faith. There is a genuine cooperation of man and God.[32]

This grace brings an awakening to man. As he cooperates with God, man can see the depths of his own sin, and this knowledge is absolutely necessary for his faith. His knowledge of his own sin which comes by way of God's grace promotes repentance, and thereby leads to faith in Christ.[33] Sin is revealed by the law. This law had been obscured by the fall of man, but God through his grace "re-inscribed the law on the heart of his dark, sinful creature."[34] So it is of grace that a man is led to repentance. Repentance is necessary to faith, but faith is the sole condition of justification. Wesley does not look upon the works of repentance as meriting salvation, but only as a condition to faith.

Works Before Justification

Are these works before justification properly good works? In his sermon, "Justification by Faith," Wesley says any works before justification cannot be good, strictly speaking. In one sense charitable works are good, but they are not good in themselves nor in the sight of

God if done before justification. As has been seen, all the good works a man may do are because of grace and are rightly of God, but strictly they are not good except after justification.

> No works are good, which are not done as God has willed and commanded them to be done.
> But no works done before justification are done as God hath willed and commanded them to be done:
> Therefore, no works done before justification are good.[35]

> A man may be of a compassionate and a benevolent temper. He may be affable, courteous, generous, and friendly. He may have some degree of meekness, patience, temperance, and of many other moral virtues. He may feel some desires of shaking off all vice, and of attaining higher degrees of virtue. He may abstain from much evil; perhaps from all that is grossly contrary to justice, mercy or truth. He may do much good, may feed the hungry, clothe the naked, relieve the widow and fatherless. He may attend public worship, use prayer in private, read many books of devotion; and yet for all this, he may be a mere natural man, knowing neither himself nor God; equally a stranger to the spirit of fear and to that of love; having neither repented, nor believed the gospel.[36]

Yet it must be remembered that Wesley would account for all these good things in an unregenerate man as coming from grace.[37] These virtues, though having the appearance of goodness, cannot be truly good until done in faith and, until then, they have the nature of sin.[38] To do a good work by the grace of God, and not acknowledge it as of God with a true faith in Jesus Christ, was wrong and not truly good.

All of Grace

It can now be seen that Wesley can rightly use the phrase, "All of grace." Even though he taught that man cooperates with God in his salvation and has the power to choose to go with God, or against Him, yet his power of cooperating and choosing is of grace. It is all of God's grace.

> The true Arminian, as fully as the Calvinist, admits the doctrine of the total depravity of human nature in consequence of the fall of our first parents; and is indeed enabled to carry it through his sys-

> tem with greater consistency than the Calvinist himself. For, while the latter is obliged, in order to account for certain good dispositions and occasional religious inclinations in those who never give any evidence of their actual conversion to God, to refer them to *nature,* and not to grace, which, according to them, is not given to the reprobate, the believer in general redemption maintains the total incapacity of unassisted nature to produce such effects, and attributes them to that Divine gracious influenced which, if not resisted, would lead on to conversion.[39]

Wesley could even believe that improving the physical health could aid a person on his way to God.[40] Education can help a person to God, and so can the means of grace.[41] One is to work out his own salvation and he must do it himself, or it will never be done. Yet it begins with preventing grace and could not be done without such.[42] For Wesley, then, all the good done before true faith, and all the efforts put forth by man toward his salvation are all of God's grace, and man would have been left hopelessly lost without that grace.

Nature Plus Grace

The man, by nature, then, is a man completely apart from the grace of God, and Wesley cannot draw that picture of man too black. But is there such a man in reality? The only man who would be such would be he who had completely stifled the grace of God. Such a man could hardly continue to exist. What becomes of Wesley's natural man, then? Dr. Lee thinks that for Wesley "the natural man is a logical abstraction." He in reality does not exist.[43] Wesley says that "there is no man that is in a state of mere nature."[44] There is in every person two contrary principles, nature and grace.[45]

> "It is a fact," says a modern writer, "that every individual has a rudimentary moral nature derived from God, the Source of all goodness, and that apart from this ethical potentiality, to which appeal can be made, moral influence and training would go for nothing." This statement depicts Wesley's position accurately.[46]

Thus Wesley preserves two important truths. First, he places proper emphasis upon proneness to evil, and second, he safeguards the initiative of God in the salvation of man.[47] One could add to these a third truth—man is considered able to cooperate with God in his own salvation. The fact that man has grace and is able to cooperate with God does not disprove the existence of the natural in man. The two facts must be seen together. Man by nature and man by grace must go hand in hand.

> This is Wesley's way of escape from the theological and psychological dilemma which the doctrine of original sin poses for all who adopt it… In this world man exists as a natural man plus the prevenient grace of God.[48]

It will now be our task to examine Wesley's concept of sin in view of these two factors that are present in the human race.

Endnotes

1. Cannon, *op. cit.*, 100.
2. *Works*, II, 237-238.
3. *Ibid.*, 435.
4. Cannon, *op. cit.*, 93.
5. *Works*, I, 482.
6. *Ibid.*, 13.
7. *Ibid.*, 482.
8. *Ibid.* V, 589.
9. *Ibid.*, 540.
10. Wiley, *op. cit.*, II, 65.
11. *Works*, I, 482.
12. R. S. Foster, *Studies in Theology*, New York: Eaton and Mains, 1899, VI, 123.
13. John Miley, *Systematic Theology*, New York: The Methodist Book Concern, 1892, II, 432.
14. *Works,* V, 196.
15. *Ibid.*, 577.
16. *Ibid.*, 647.
17. Watson, *op. cit.*, II, 59.
18. *Works*, VII, 97.
19. Lee, *op. cit.*, 125.
20. *Works*, II, 118.
21. *Ibid.*, 37-43.

22. *Ibid.*, V, 547.
23. Cannon, *op. cit.*, 106-108.
24. *Works*, VI, 42.
25. *Ibid.*, II, 128-129.
26. *Ibid.*, 377-379.
27. *Ibid.*, 47.
28. Watson, *op. cit.*, II, 61.
29. *Works*, II, 73.
30. *Ibid.*, V, 541.
31. John Wesley, *Explanatory Notes Upon the New Testament*, London: The Epworth Press, 1948, 520-525. (Now available from Schmul Publishing Co., Nicholasville, KY.)
32. Cannon, *op. cit.*, 114-115.
33. *Works*, V, 574.
34. *Ibid.*, I, 308.
35. *Ibid.*, 49.
36. *Ibid.*, 84.
37. Watson, *op. cit.*, II, 85. See also Henry Wheeler, *History and Exposition of the Twenty-five Articles of Religion of the Methodist Episcopal Church*, New York: Eaton and Mains, 1908, 25-26. Wheeler believes Wesley saw a problem in making works before justification to be of the nature of sin, while at the same time ascribing them to God's grace. So Wesley left out the article of the Church of England dealing with works before justification in his revision.
38. *Works*, III, 152-154.
39. Watson, *op. cit.*, II, 48.
40. Prince, *op. cit.*, 24.
41. *Works*, I, 143.
42. *Ibid.*, 235.
43. Lee, *op. cit.*, 124.
44. *Works*, II, 238.
45. *Ibid.*, I, 115.
46. Prince, *op. cit.*, 38. Quote from Mackintosh, *The Divine Initiative*, 86.
47. Lee, *op. cit.*, 125-126.
48. *Ibid.*, 124-125.

Chapter 7

The Nature of Sin—Willful

THUS FAR IN THIS BOOK we have noticed that Wesley considered that the fall of man was occasioned by the willful choice of the original parents. This original sin was passed on to their posterity so that everyone is born with a sinful nature from which proceeds evil fruit. This sinful condition in mankind can only be explained by the fact that all are born with a sinful nature. Along with this sinful nature with which men are born is superadded the prevenient grace of God. By this grace a man is better than he would be if left alone with his nature.

In discussing the nature of sin as seen by Wesley it will be helpful to make some careful distinctions. His concept of sin is best seen as he applies it to three general classes of individuals. In the sinner one can see the willfulness in sin. In the believer who is justified and regenerated, but not fully sanctified, one can see the principle of sin. In the entirely sanctified it is possible to observe the infirmities, improperly called sins. This chapter will deal with the nature of sin as it is revealed in willfulness. The next two chapters will contain a discussion of sin as principle and infirmity, respectively.

Definition

It has already been noticed that Adam was holy in nature before he was holy in act.[1] However, he had the power of choice and could choose evil, which he did. There were two steps in his sin. He became unholy before he committed an unholy act. First, there were pride and unbelief as inward sins before there was the actual act of disobedience.[2] The fall was first internal, then external.[3]

Although Adam was the cause of his own internal sin as well as the external, present man is born with an internal sinfulness out of which he commits his own sins, and makes the internal sinfulness his own. The sinful state precedes the sinful act.[4] Man is not responsible for the sinful condition in which he is born, but he is responsible for the acts of sin which proceed from this sinfulness.

Wesley's definition of sin as a voluntary transgression is well known. In a letter in 1772 he wrote,

> Nothing is sin, strictly speaking, but a voluntary transgression of the known law of God. Therefore, every voluntary breach of the law of love is sin; and nothing else, if we speak properly. To strain the matter farther is only to make way for Calvinism. There may be ten thousand wandering thoughts, and forgetful intervals, without any breach of love, though not without transgressing the Adamic law. But Calvinism would fain confound these together. Let love fill your heart, and that is enough![5]

Here Wesley makes the only properly-called sin to be voluntary, or willful. It is either the willful committing of an act that is known to be wrong, or the consenting to an inward temper that is evil. Wesley believes that this definition is the only Scriptural one and, although every sin is a transgression of the law, it does not follow that every transgression of a law is sin.[6] Two things are, therefore, true for an act to be sin. There must, first, be a knowledge of the law and, second, the disobedience is willful. Wesley defines this same kind of sin as follows:

> By sin, I here understand outward sin, according to the plain common acceptation of the word; an actual voluntary transgression of the law; of the revealed, written law of God; of any commandment of God, acknowledged to be such at the time it is transgressed.[7]

This above quotation from Wesley is his comment on the scripture in I John 3:9 which reads, "Whosoever is born of God doth not commit sin." This sin defined as voluntary is what the believer who is born of God does not commit.[8] As will be seen later, the believer does have sin all right, but of a different kind. He does not commit willful sin; in fact he cannot commit such a sin and remain in a justified state.

Wesley also recognized there is a principle of sin that is distinct from the willful act. This is the sin with which men are born. He accepts the Ninth Article of the Church of England which, he says, "exactly copies after the primitive" church.

> "...Original sin is the corruption of the nature of every man, whereby man is in his own nature inclined to evil, so that the flesh lusteth contrary to the spirit. And this infection of nature doth remain, yea in them that are regenerated, whereby the lust of the flesh... is not subject to the law of God."[9]

Wesley calls this remaining "infection of our nature" an "inward sin." It consists of "any sinful temper, passion, or affection." It is any "deposition contrary to the mind which was in Christ," such as "pride, self will, love of the world," and "lust, anger, peevishness."[10] The believer does not give any voluntary consent to these inward sins, so does not commit sin in the proper sense. Yet the believer is sinful and feels the inward sins.

Flew recognizes that Wesley had a two-fold definition of sin, but failed to distinguish between the inward sin and the sins of infirmity.[11] This third class of sins, "improperly so-called," are those defects that remain with the sanctified who no longer have the remains of the inbred sin. They are not "condemned for *sins of infirmity,"* nor for *"involuntary failings,"* nor for anything that they cannot help. These things that one cannot avoid are neither of a willful nature, nor are they inward sins which can be cleansed.[12]

Turner in his book, *The More Excellent Way,* sees that in Wesley sin has a three-fold aspect. He calls this third class "sins of ignorance." But these "sins of ignorance" are the "sins of infirmity" that grow out of human ignorance.[13] Failure to see this three-fold aspect of sin in Wesley's concept has created much confusion. Tennant, in his *The Concept of Sin,* makes sin only of the one kind, the willful.[14] Sangster thinks that Wesley and Tennant agree in their concept of willful sin and that Wesley would agree with Tennant that there is no such thing as "unconscious sin."[15] Yet it is clear that Wesley saw that the sin remaining in believers was not always easily detected. Sangster seems to have failed to observe carefully Wesley's sermon, "On Sin in Believers."[16] These distinctions will be dealt with at length in the next two chapters.

Personal Sin

This sin which Wesley defines as voluntary is of a personal nature. It is committed by the individual and is an act. It is not only an external act, but also internal and personal, "an act of the soul itself, in determining itself by free choice to that which it knows to be in violation of law. The sin consists in this primary act of the will."[17] The act is not necessitated; it is a free act of the individual. The prevenient grace lifts man to the place that he can resist the sin. Therefore he is accountable. By grace man could avoid all sin.[18]

When man reaches the age of accountability, his choice of evil makes the inbred sin his own.[19] Even though it is of grace that he can avoid the sin, yet he is held accountable for consenting to the sin, for man is free.[20] Even though these sins proceed from the original sin with which he is born, man is responsible for them.[21] There can be no virtue or vice except when they are chosen.[22] When man chooses to follow the evil within him, he becomes a sinner, and has personal guilt for both his act and for the consenting to the evil within. In this sense the actual, personal sin is both external and internal.[23]

Now these personal sins are sprouts from the root that is planted within the man.[24] They become personal sins when yielded to by a moral agent. An infant or a brute, although possessing an evil nature, cannot be personal sinners because they are not capable of moral choice.[25] So a man is not a sinner in this sense until he has "personally made himself such by a free personal transgression of law."[26]

It is at this point that Wesley differs with Calvinism. He did place the affections under the will, as did Edwards. Wesley placed liberty as separate from the will.[27] Calvinism designs "to locate sin in the disposition, or inclination, or desire, back of every volitionary act, but to connect it with the will by identifying these states with the will." The purpose for this is to make man responsible for his inherited disposition, and thus to prove the guilt of all.[28] This system involves everyone personally with the guilt of Adam's sin, and justifies God in his condemnation of infants for original sin only. But Wesley makes voluntary sin to be only that committed by a personal agent who is capable of moral choice.

Sin and Punishment

Wesley did look upon all sufferings of the human race as punishments for Adam's sin. However, he did distinguish between guilt as a liability to punishment, which could be imputed to posterity, and guilt as personal. Foster sees guilt only as attaching to the person who commits the sin and he alone is guilty.[29] He recognizes that Wesley and Watson used the term *guilt* in the other sense, but declares their idea was very different from the Calvinistic.[30] To this Pope agrees, and points out that sin is an abuse of freedom and is a voluntary separation from God. He sees guilt as a personal responsibility in the sense that the sin is a personal fault and will be punished as such.[31] Wesley sees eternal punishment as reserved only for those whose sin is personal.[32]

The only kind of a sin then that can send a person into eternal punishment is that which can be classified personal. In discussing the proposition that all men are justly liable for all punishments in this world and the one to come, Wesley said, "That all men are liable to these for Adam's sin alone, I do not assert; but they are so, for their own outward and inward sins, which, through their own fault, spring from the infection of their nature."[33] He describes presumptuous sins as "open rebellion."

> The wilful sinner is not ignorant nor surprised, but knowingly fights against God's express commandment, and the lively, full, and present conviction of his own mind and conscience; so that this is the very standard of iniquity.[34]

Although there are degrees in the intensity of this rebellion, only these sins of the will can be denominated "voluntary transgressions," and they alone can cause a person to lose his soul eternally.

The Sins of the Unbeliever

Wesley likens the sinner to the unborn baby. He feels not; he sees not; he hears not. Before he is born again, he is not sensible of God. He does not hear God call; utter darkness covers his soul. There may be the beginnings of spiritual motion, but his spiritual senses are dead.[35] A man in this state commits sin with every breath he draws and "whose actual transgressions, in word and deed, are more in number than the hairs of his head."[36] This man is called the *"natural man."* He has not yet been awakened to his lost condition. He does not fear his coming punishment. He feels secure in himself. He does not see that he is a sinner. Even men of learning are in this class, and their ignorance of God "strongly glares."[37]

This unawakened sinner still is the servant of sin. "He remains a willing servant of sin content with the bondage of corruption. He is inwardly and outwardly unholy and satisfied therewith."[38] The man classified as *"under the law"* is the sinner awakened. He sees his sin and strives to put it off. But he is in prison and cannot escape. He repents and sins again. Romans, chapter seven, becomes a picture of him. His only victory is in Christ.[39] "Under grace" he can have victory.

Now Wesley classes this "natural man" as sinning willingly, the one "under the law" as sinning unwillingly, and the one "under grace" as not sinning at all.

> Art thou daily fighting against all sin, and daily more than conqueror? I acknowledge thee for a child of God. Oh stand fast in thy glorious liberty! Art thou fighting, but not conquering; striving for the mastery, but not able to attain? Then thou art not yet a believer in Christ; but follow on and thou shalt know the Lord. Art thou not fighting at all, but leading an easy, indolent, fashionable life? Oh how hast thou dared to name the name of Christ, only to make it a reproach among the heathen? Awake, thou sleeper! Call upon thy God, before the deep swallow thee up![40]

Wesley seems to hold out hope for the struggling sinner who sins unwillingly, but there is none for the sleeping one while he sleeps. Wesley does admit that all three of these states are "often mingled together, and in some measure meet in one and the same person."[41] At least this point is clear, only the one who is asleep, and sins willingly, is lost and in danger of eternal death. Wesley classified his own experience prior to his conversion in 1738 as "under the law" and a state of unwilling sinning. Soon after his conversion he stated he was not a Christian before 1738. However, he later revised his statement with "I am not sure of this." He felt he did have the faith of a servant though not of a son.[42]

The Willful Sin of the Believer

Wesley believed that a true believer could again commit willful sin and be lost eternally. To note his description as to how this can happen in a believer helps to see the nature of willful sin. As indicated above, the believer does not commit willful sin. In fact he cannot commit sin "so long as that seed remaineth in him." But he observes that such sins were committed by men such as David, Barnabas, and Peter. How does the believer fall?

> It is easy therefore to understand, how any of these children of God might be moved from his own steadfastness, and yet the great truth of God, declared by the apostle, remain steadfast and unshaken. He did not "keep himself," by that grace of God which was sufficient for him. He fell, step by step, first into negative, inward sin, not "stirring up the gift of God which was in him," not "watching unto prayer," not "pressing on to the mark of the prize of his high calling;" then into positive inward sin, inclining to wickedness with his heart, giving way to some evil desire or temper. Next, he lost his faith, his sight of a pardoning God, and consequently his love of God: and, being then weak and like another man, he was capable of committing even outward sin.[43]

In answering the question whether faith is lost before one can commit a sin, or whether one's willful sin causes the loss of faith, Wesley answers, "Some sin of omission, at least, must necessarily precede the loss of faith; some inward sin: but the loss of faith must precede the committing outward sin."[44] In discussing sins of surprise which come with a sudden and violent temptation, Wesley can see that there may be more or less of guilt or condemnation according to the degree of the concurrence of the will. However, if a man had passed by a previous warning by "wilful and culpable neglect" and then, later, is taken unawares, he is without excuse. "The falling, even by surprise, in such an instance as this, is, in effect, a wilful sin; and, as such, must expose the sinner to condemnation, both from God and his own conscience." Yet there is no need that a man ever give in to such sins if he is on his guard.[45]

Repentance and Forgiveness

For these willful acts of sin the sinner must repent in order to be forgiven. The way into the kingdom is by repentance and faith. "Know thyself to be a sinner, and what manner of sinner thou art." See the corruption, the darkness, the ignorance, the perverseness, "the wounds, and bruises, and putrefying sores." From this root one should see the branches that grow, such as unbelief, independence, pride, vanity, wrong desires, tempers and lusts. And all these lead to "hell fire." In fact one is already "under the sentence of hell fire."[46] Wesley exhorts the backslider to recognize if he has committed any sin that has grieved the Holy Spirit and to put away the "accursed thing."[47]

Repentance leads to faith and forgiveness. One is justified by faith alone, but repentance is a condition of faith. Wesley distinguishes between justification and sanctification. While sanctification is being made just and righteous and is a real change, justification "is pardon, the forgiveness of sins." God will not condemn the sinner; his sins will not be imputed to him. "His sins, all his past sins, in thought, word, and deed, are covered, are blotted out, shall not be remembered or mentioned against him, anymore than if they had not been."[48] Thus it is clear that Wesley saw justification as forgiveness for these willful sins that had brought guilt to the sinner, and had subjected him to the threat of eternal death. It is a work that is done for us and takes away the guilt of sin, but not its power or defilement.[49] Pardon is needed for the guilt but cleansing for the defilement.[50]

No sin could be so great but what it could be forgiven. Wesley held out hope for the lowest. The sin of "blasphemy against the Holy Ghost" was a special kind of sin, and no one need fear his having committed it. The "sin unto death" did not refer to eternal death so could not preclude forgiveness.[51] For the worst of sinners and for the man who had backslidden, there was forgiveness through repentance and faith.

Willful sin, therefore, is committed only by the unbeliever who is capable of free choice. An infant has not committed such a sin so needs no forgiveness. Their salvation consists in the salvation from the guilt of Adam's sin so is not the same as justification by faith.[52] No believer commits a willful sin while he is a believer, but he can lose his faith. These willful sins are the only ones that can send a person to hell. Our task now is to observe more closely the principle of sin as is seen in the believer.

Endnotes

1. *Works,* V, 561.
2. *Ibid*., II, 32.
3. Pope, *op. cit.* II, 15.
4. *Works*, V, 570, 593.
5. *Ibid*., VII, 56.
6. *Ibid*., II, 172.
7. *Ibid*., I, 164.
8. *Ibid*., 166.
9. *Ibid*., 108.
10. *Ibid.,* 109.
11. Flew, *op. cit.* 326.
12. *Works*, I, 74.
13. Turner, *op. cit.* 238.
14. F.R. Tennant, *The Concept Sin*. Cambridge: University Press, 1912. 104-105.
15. W. E. Sangster, *The Path to Perfection*. New York: Abingdon-Cokesbury Press, 1943, 71-72.
16. Turner, *op. cit.* 237-238.
17. Foster, *op. cit.* VI, 33.
18. *Works*, V, 575, 593.
19. *Ibid*., 548.
20. *Ibid*., II, 39. See also Burtner and Chiles, *op. cit.,* 132.
21. *Ibid*., 475-476.
23. *Works*, *op. cit.,* II, 68.
24. Lindstrom, *op. cit.*, 38.
25. *Works*, V, 584.
26. Foster, *op. cit.,* VI, 31.
27. Turner, *op. cit.,* 234.
28. Foster, *op. cit.,* VI, 28.
29. *Ibid*., 117.
30. *Ibid*., 183.
31. Pope, *op. cit.,* II, 27-36.

32. *Works*, I, 65, 241.
34. *Ibid.*, II, 518.
35. *Ibid.*, I, 162-163.
36. *Ibid.*, 58.
37. *Ibid.*, 76-77.
38. *Ibid.*, 78.
39. *Ibid.*, 79-81.
40. *Ibid.*, 83.
41. *Ibid.*, sec. 2.
42. Lee, *op. cit.*, 97.
43. *Works*, I, 165-166.
44. *Ibid.*, 168.
45. *Ibid.*, 72-74.
46. *Ibid.*, 64-65.
47. *Ibid.*, 413-414.
48. *Ibid.*, 47-48.
49. *Ibid.*, 162.
50. Turner, *op. cit.,* 247.
51. *Works*, II, 243-246.
52. *Ibid.,* VII, 97.

Chapter 8

The Nature of Sin—Principle

In the last chapter we saw that Wesley had a concept of sin known as a willful act. This kind of sin involves a free choice and carries personal responsibility. An examination will now be made of Wesley's view of sin as a principle, or state, especially as it is found in the believer. It must be distinguished from character which has become sinful because of the tree choices of the individual. The sinner by his choices becomes an habitual sinner and sin reigns in his life. This is all included in the outward and inward aspects of willful sin and is dealt with in the experience of justification and regeneration. The principle of sin is that with which one is born and which remains in the believer after justification.

Definition

It has been made clear that Wesley believed that all men are born with an evil nature, which is a deprivation resulting from the absence of moral likeness to God and a depravation resulting from the deprivation. This depravity is an inclination, or propensity, to sin and is a total corruption of man's nature. Although it is alleviated more or less by prevenient grace, since man is not in a state of mere nature, yet every individual possesses this principle of evil.

For this principle of sin within himself a man is not personally responsible, nor guilty, until he makes it his own by personal choice. Yet this principle is of the nature of sin and can be called sinful. It has been noted that Wesley believed that men are sinners because of this nature but in a special sense. They were not sinners in the personal sense but only in the sense that they are accounted guilty of Adam's sin in that he was their representative, and they are punished for his sin. However, this guilt is removed through the prevenient grace of God, and man is not responsible for his evil nature until, by rejection of the remedy, he "ratifies it as his own."[1]

Now this principle of sin, or inbeing of sin, or inbred sin, or infection of nature, does remain in those that are justified. Its power is broken, but it is not expelled from the heart. Sooner or later it will manifest itself, and the believer will become conscious that his heart is still evil. However, this evil does not reign and the believer is able to be an overcomer.

Wesley deals with this subject at length and quite thoroughly in his sermons, "Sin in Believers," and "Repentance of Believers." These were especially written to contest the error of Count Zinzendorf and the English Moravians who held that the being of sin no longer remained in them that are believers. Wesley believed that this error was held only by the English Moravians.[2]

As already noted, Wesley defined this sin according to the Ninth Article as the infection of nature that remained in the regenerated.

> By sin, I here understand inward sin; any sinful temper, passion, or affection; such as pride, self will, love of the world, in any kind or degree; such as lust, anger, peevishness; any disposition contrary to the mind which was in Christ.

He feels this doctrine is as old as the church, and was held for seventeen hundred years until Count Zinzendorf discovered his new theory. Because it was new, it must be wrong.[3]

Wesley draws a very clear distinction in defining the words *guilt, power,* and *being*. He says they are not the same thing. "That believers are delivered from the *guilt* and *power* of sin we allow; that they are delivered from the being of it we deny."[4] This "being" of sin is that which remains after justification although Wesley does teach that it can be destroyed in entire sanctification. This remaining sin, or "inbred sin" will persist in the believer until it pleases God to speak the second time, and then "inbred sin subsists no more."[5]

How does Wesley's position stand along with the other creeds?

> The council of Trent declared: (Tr. by Sugden) There remains in the

> baptized concupiscence or the fuel (of sin). This concupiscence, which sometimes the Apostle calls sin, the Holy Synod declares that the Catholic Church has never understood to be called sin because it is truly and properly sin in the regenerate, but because it arises from sin and inclines to sin.
>
> The Westminster Confession (IV, 5), on the contrary, asserts: This corruption of nature during this life doth remain in those that are regenerated, and although it be through Christ pardoned and mortified, yet both itself, and all the motions thereof, are truly and properly sin. The Augsburg Confession says of the corruption of human nature: Nor is it by any means abolished or done away by baptism, since sin always issues forth from this woeful source, as water from a fountain.[6]

Wesley would seem to be a mediator between these two contrasting statements. Where he agrees with the Tridentine statement that this remaining sin is not sin in the true and proper sense, he agrees with the Westminster position that it is a corruption of nature. He would not agree that the sins that issue forth from this remaining pollution are true and proper sins, but that they are sinful and need cleansing.

Flew, in *The Idea of Perfection,* thinks Wesley has defects in his theory of perfection, and that these defects grow out of an inadequate analysis of the nature of sin. He thinks Wesley's definition of sin as a voluntary transgression is too limited, and the stress on the "consciousness and deliberate intention of the agent is the most formidable defect in Wesley's doctrine of the ideal." He further adds that Wesley's "stress on the instantaneous nature of the deliverance masks a deficient analysis of the nature of moral evil in traditional theology."[7] We shall examine to see if there is this deficiency.

Tennant, in addition to defining sin as a volitional act, describes the primitive emotions in man, but denies that they can be sin. His evolutionary opinions caused him to discard the theory of original sin. Thus, he thought there could be no such thing as "unconscious sin."[8] Sangster is quite insistent in classing Wesley as agreeable to Tennant. He emphasizes Wesley's one definition of sin as conscious, or willful, but fails to indicate that Wesley's concept of sin as a principle is revealed in the heart of the believer.[9] Turner thinks that both Flew and Sangster are wrong in their understanding of Wesley's position.[10] Lee recognizes that Wesley had a concept of sin as an inherent disposition toward evil, as distinct from evil acts, but he thinks that Wesley looked upon that principle as a substance.[11] In the remaining sections of this chapter we shall examine Wesley's view as to the nature of inward sin.

The Root of All Sin

Evidence has already been given to show that Wesley saw something deeper in man than the outward wickedness that can be seen. It was the root of all sin and is found in every man. This original sin is atheism, which is an absence of any knowledge of God and an inclination to depart from God. It takes the form of idolatry so that man makes himself into his own god. He is born a rank idolater.[12] This inner sin is a disease likened to leprosy.[13] This disease needs to be healed.[14] These diseases are atheism, idolatry, pride, love of the world, anger and deviation from the truth.[15] Now all of these are sins in the heart even before choices can be made.

Wesley understands Paul in his use of the word "flesh" to be referring to this inward principle. "The flesh, in the usual language of St. Paul, signifies corrupt nature."[16] When Taylor attempts to make flesh refer only to the body, Wesley reduces the idea to an absurdity by quoting certain Scripture texts.[17] This flesh is not located in the body, but in the soul.[18] It is born in man, is in the sinner, and remains in the believer.[19]

Since this flesh is located in the soul of man, how could it be a thing, or "substance," in Wesley's mind? The spirit is not made up of material, so sin in the heart, or spirit, could not be a thing. Also, Wesley's idea that sin could be removed, or destroyed, argues against the idea that it was substance. It was this very belief that sin could be removed that caused him to differ with the Reformers. He did not believe this inward sin was so bound up with the flesh that it could not be eliminated.[20] Spirit alone can sin, or be sinful.

> For no *body,* or matter of any kind, can be *sinful:* spirits alone are capable of sin. Pray in what part of the body should it lodge? It cannot

> lodge in the skin, nor in the muscles, or nerves, or veins, or arteries; it cannot be in the bones, any more than in the hair or nails. Only the soul can be the seat of sin.[21]

So it is quite wrong to look upon Wesley as seeing sin as a thing or substance. If his terms mislead his readers, the fault will lie in the fact that he uses Scriptural terms. When his ideas are carefully read, there is no need to interpret his concept of sin as a thing.

Sin in Believers

It will be of interest at this point to examine more closely Wesley's sermons, "Sin in Believers" and "Repentance of Believers." This believer, or justified person, is born again. He is a child of God and his body is a temple of the Holy Spirit. He is washed and sanctified. His heart is purified and he worships in spirit and truth. He keeps the commandments, and has power over all sin from the moment he is justified.

However, this believer is not freed from all sin. When the Apostle says, "The flesh lusteth against the Spirit, and the Spirit against the flesh: these are contrary the one to the other," he "directly affirms that the flesh, evil nature, opposes the Spirit, even in believers; that even in the regenerate, there are two principles, 'contrary the one to the other.'" He sees the church at Corinth as a justified people, yet carnal. The Bible clearly teaches that in believers there are two contrary principles, "nature and grace, the flesh and Spirit."[22] Concerning the experience of Christians, he writes,

> These continually feel a heart bent to backsliding; a natural tendency to evil; a proneness to depart from God, and cleave to the things of earth. They are daily sensible of sin remaining in their heart, pride, self will, unbelief; and of sin cleaving to all they speak and do, even their best actions and holiest duties. Yet at the same time they "know that they are of God..."[23]

How can a man have pride or anger in him, and yet not be angry or proud? Wesley answers that one may have pride and even think of himself more than he ought to think, and not be a proud man in his general character. He says that "some pride and anger may be in that heart, where there is much humility and meekness." Resentment is a sin because it does not conform to the law of love, but it need not reign. If resentment is felt, but not yielded to, there is no guilt nor condemnation. There can be sin without guilt or power.[24]

Wesley does not see believers proud or self-willed in the same way that unbelievers are. The sinner is governed by them and obeys sin, but the believer does not. The sinner "walks after the flesh" while the believer "walks after the Spirit," although both have "flesh" in them. *"Having sin* does not forfeit the favor of God; *giving way to sin* does."[25] In Wesley's mind there was a vast difference between the willful sin of the sinner, and the principle of sin in the believer. Not to see this distinction comes from a misreading of Wesley.

Repentance and Cleansing

Wesley gives an important place to the repentance that is necessary before the faith by which we are justified. It is a conviction of our utter sinfulness, guiltiness, and helplessness. There is another kind of repentance, in addition to this initial kind. This latter repentance is as essential, along with faith, for the continuance and growth in grace, as the former was in entering the kingdom.[26]

This repentance for believers is a form of self-knowledge. It is a conviction of the sin that "remains." "It does not reign, but it does remain." The believer realizes that there is still pride, self-will, idolatry, pride of life, desire of the eye, jealousies, evil surmisings, envy, and covetousness. It is the believer who is not thus convicted who is unconscious of these sins in his life. The sin is there whether it is seen or not. The teaching that we are fully cleansed at justification cuts off all watching against the "Delilah" in our bosom, and leaves one exposed to the assaults of the enemy. This "root of bitterness," this "depth of corruption," cannot possibly be seen without the clear light of God.[27] Sangster's criticism that Wesley did not believe in an "unconscious sin" will hardly stand the test of these statements. Wesley would agree with Flew that sometimes the worst sins of the believer are unconscious although Flew thought Wesley had no such concept.[28]

This deep repentance for the indwelling sin in the heart of the believer was necessary for the cleansing. One must see himself as guilty of numerous sins, such as are seen in the seventh chapter of Romans. He will see sin cleaving to his actions. There will be numerous inward defects. Now for these one is guilty. The believer must be convicted of this guilt. Wesley guards this point carefully and says it must be cautiously understood in a peculiar sense. Yet these inward sins cannot bear the rigors of the strict justice of God. They do deserve punishment and would absolutely condemn were it not for the atoning blood. "They still deserve, strictly speaking, only the damnation of hell. But what they deserve does not come upon them, because they 'have an advocate with the Father.'"[29]

As far as inward sins are concerned, it may seem at first from the above that there is little difference between those of the sinner and those of the believer, except that the believer's cannot condemn him. However, one must remember that for Wesley the sinner is consenting to his and willingly sins, while the believer is fighting against his and they do not reign in his life. Also the sinner's sins are allowed to become outward while such is not true for the justified.

In order to be cleansed the believer must not only feel the inward sin, and be convinced of his guiltiness and demerit for them, but he also must realize his utter helplessness to deliver himself. He cannot expel his "pride, self-will, or inbred sin in general." With the grace he has already received, it cannot be done. One may weaken his enemies, but he cannot drive them out. To realize this is an essential point with Wesley. One not deeply convinced of his corruption and utter helplessness will have little concern for cleansing. One cannot groan for deliverance until he know himself, until "God unveils the inbred monster's face" and shows him his real state. It is then they cry out for the yoke to be broken. God speaks the second time and "inbred sin subsists no more."[30]

Sin and Perfect Love

It is not designed in this book to examine Wesley's view on Christian perfection. However, one can understand his concept of the nature of the sin which remains after justification better to see it in the light of perfect love. Anything short of the ideal of perfect love is wrong and sinful.

> If we set our affection on things of the earth, on any person or thing under the sun; if we desire anything but God; and what tends to God, if we seek happiness in any creature; the jealous God will surely contend with us, for he can admit of no rival.[31]

In opposition to the external righteousness of the Pharisees, Wesley sees the righteousness of the Christian which is to exceed that of the Pharisees by being internal. It includes "poverty of spirit, mourning, meekness, hunger and thirst after righteousness, the love of our neighbor, and purity of heart."[32] In further description of this inward righteousness, Wesley writes,

> Let thy religion be the religion of the heart. Be thou poor in spirit, little, and base, and mean, and vile in thy own eyes: amazed and humbled to the dust at the love of God which is in Christ Jesus thy Lord! Be serious: let the whole stream of thy thoughts, words, and works, be such as flows from the deepest conviction that thou standest on the edge of the great gulf, thou, and all the children of men, just ready to drop in, either into everlasting glory or everlasting burnings! Be meek: let thy soul be filled with mildness, gentleness, patience, longsuffering towards all men: at the same time that all which is in thee is athirst for God, longing to awake up after his likeness, and to be satisfied with it. Be thou a lover of God, and of all mankind. In this spirit do, and suffer all things.[33]

In another description of this love Wesley describes it as "love excluding sin, love filling the heart, taking up the whole capacity of the soul. It is love 'rejoicing evermore, praying without ceasing, in everything giving thanks.'"[34] Now this is the ideal that Wesley set up as the goal for every Christian, and that could be attained in this life in the experience of entire sanctification. Anything short of this law of perfect love would be sinful and a mark of the carnal mind. Anything short of true justifying faith and complete reliance on Christ for forgiveness would be willful sinning.

It is now possible to conclude that Wesley draws a clear distinction between outward, willful transgression of the law of God, and an inward state, or principle, that results from the corruption of our natures. The first deserves the punishment from God, and will receive eternal death unless the person is justified. The second, though deserving of punishment, is not condemning because of the atonement in Christ. But it needs the cleansing offered in Christ. The first comes as a result of personal volition; the second, by birth with an infected nature. The first is to be forgiven; the second, to be purged.[35]

Our next step is to examine what Wesley taught about that which is left after the purging. It may resemble sin and is often called sin. To this we now turn in the next chapter.

Endnotes

1. Wiley, *op. cit.*, II, 137.
2. *Works*, I, 108.
3. *Ibid.*, 109-111.
4. *Ibid.*, 113.
5. *Ibid.*, 121-122.
6. Sugden, *op. cit.*, I, 262-263.
7. Flew, *op. cit.*, 332-334.
8. Tennant, *op. cit.*, 129-131.
9. Sangster, *op. cit.*, 72-75.
10. Turner, *op. cit.*, 239.
11. Lee, *op. cit.*, 122.
12. *Works*, I, 395.
13. *Ibid.*, 82.
14. *Ibid.*, II, 435.
15. *Ibid.*, 309-310.
16. *Ibid.*, I, 69.
17. *Ibid.*, V, 553.
18. *Ibid.*, 635.
19. *Ibid.*, I, 115.
20. Turner, *op. cit.*, 249.
21. *Works*, II, 172.
22. *Ibid.*, I, 108-110.
23. *Ibid.*, 110.
24. *Ibid.*, 114.
25. *Ibid.*, 115.
26. *Ibid.*, 116.
27. *Ibid.*, 117-119.

28. Flew, *op. cit.*, 332-333.
29. *Works*, I, 120-121.
30. *Ibid.,* 121-125.
31. *Ibid.,* 411.
32. *Ibid.,* 231.
33. *Ibid.,* 232.
34. *Ibid.,* 386.
35. *Ibid.,* 47-48, 114, 121-122; V, 301-303.

Chapter 9

The Nature of Sin—Infirmity

WESLEY TOOK MUCH TIME to clarify his teachings concerning perfection because they had created so much opposition and misunderstanding. Those who opposed the teaching often accused Wesley of teaching a kind of perfection that he did not teach, so it became necessary for him to make careful distinctions on the subject. One of his major works on this subject was the *Plain Account of Christian Perfection,* in which he deals quite at length with the difference between the sin from which one is cleansed in sanctification, and the infirmities, or mistakes, that remain in the entirely sanctified.

It is in the teaching of perfection, especially a kind that would be attainable in this life, that such distinctions would become necessary. For one not teaching a perfection attainable in this life, a distinction between sins of infirmity, or ignorance, and the sins of evil tempers, such as pride, might not be too important. But for Wesley such distinction was of vast importance. The reason for this importance would be self-evident. One could not know they had attained unless they could know what could still remain, and yet be consistent with perfect love.

Definition

Wesley did not like to contend, but his position as leader in a movement committed to the doctrine of Christian perfection made it necessary for him often to do so. When others claimed "that coming short is sin," Wesley answers, "I contend not." Yet he goes ahead to declare that those who have perfect love are "cleansed from all sin."[1] When some advised that he drop the words, "perfect," and "perfection," because they caused offense, he answered, "Are they not found in the oracles of God?" He felt no one had a right to lay aside the words of God. It was their duty to explain the meaning of them. And this explaining he attempts to do.[2]

Now Wesley could believe that all sin is a transgression of the law, but he could not believe that all transgression of the law is sin.[3] He doubted if "sins of infirmity" should be called sin.

> Perhaps it were advisable rather to call them *infirmities,* that we may not seem to give any countenance to sin, or to extenuate it in any degree, by thus coupling it with infirmity. But (if we must retain so ambiguous and dangerous an expression.) by sins of infirmity I would mean, such involuntary failings, as the saying a thing we believe true, though, in fact, it prove to be false; or the hurting our neighbor without knowing or designing it, perhaps when we designed to do him good. Though these arc deviations from the holy, and acceptable, and perfect will of God, yet they are not properly sins, nor do they bring any guilt on the conscience of "them that are in Christ Jesus." They separate not between God and them, neither intercept the light of his countenance, as being no ways inconsistent with their general character of "walking not after the flesh, but after the Spirit."[4]

Because of these infirmities, Wesley did not wish to use the term *sinless perfection.* Although infirmities were not properly sins since they do not violate the law of love, yet they could be sins since they were short of God's perfect law, and could not bear the "rigor of God's justice," but needed "the atoning blood."[5] It is important in Wesleyan thought to observe the distinction in these two laws.[6] Fletcher makes this distinction very clear in an answer to a Mr. Hill.

> Should Mr. Hill ask if the Christian perfection which we contend for, is a *sinless* perfection, we reply, Sin is the transgression of a Divine law, and man may be considered either as being under the *anti-evangelical, Christless, remediless law of our Creator;* or, as being under the *evangelical, mediatorial, remedying law of our Redeemer:* and the question must be answered according to the nature of these two laws.
>
> With respect to the first, that is, the Adamic, Christless law of innocence and paradisiacal perfection, we utterly renounce the doctrine of sinless perfection… Our mental and bodily powers are so enfeebled, that we cannot help actually breaking *that* law in numberless instances, even after our full conversion. …Therefore, I repeat it, with respect to the Christless law of paradisiacal obedience, we entirely disclaim *sinless*

> perfection; and, improperly speaking, we say with Luther, "In every good work the just man sinneth;"... But Christ has so completely fulfilled Creator's paradisiacal law of innocence, which allows neither of repentance nor of renewed obedience, that we shall not be judged by that law, but by a law adapted to our present state and circumstances, a milder law, called "the law of Christ," i.e. the Mediator's law, which is, like himself, "full of evangelical grace and truth."[7]

It is clear then that all deviations that come between that law of love and that perfect law can be classed as infirmities or mistakes, and are not sin in any proper sense.

Consequent to the Fall

In discussing the consequences of the fall it has already been noted how mankind lost because Adam did not keep his first estate. The evil that came into the world was not only the sinfulness that was passed on to man but also the many misfortunes that come upon the human race. Wesley saw these as penal consequences of Adam's sin in that the race does suffer punishment for original sin. Now these punishments are not removed even when man turns to Christ and receives of His grace. A comparison of what Wesley thought the world was like before the fall and what it became like afterwards reveals the condition to which man is subjected and from which there is no deliverance in this life.

These effects of sin are called the "scars of sin." The broken vessel has been mended sufficiently to get us through this life, but it will not have the ring of Adamic perfection while in this earth.[8] This humanity we possess is called an "earthen vessel," and shall be such no matter how much we regain the "image of God" wherein we were created.[9] It is a broken humanity, but a broken humanity is not of necessity sinful.[10] This brokenness is a result of the disease that was in the nature. The disease is gone, but the after-effects remain.[11]

This loss through the fall that is not of a sinful nature includes a disordered world. The ground has been cursed. It includes a mortal, corruptible body which at best serves man imperfectly.[12] We are subjected to ten thousand sufferings, both from our own bodies, and from the world we live in.[13] These losses are the work of the devil from which man is to be delivered in Christ, but all the deliverance does not come in this life.[14] We would have much to keep us reminded that we are members of a fallen race even if all were fully sanctified.

Depravity of the Body

Wesley believed that the soul of man was depraved and that the sinful nature was in the soul. Did he believe that the body was also depraved? He calls it the "corruptible body" through which the soul must operate, and that it, with its organs, is "more debased and depraved by the fall of man, than we can possibly conceive." Also the brain suffers with the rest of the body.[15] Dr. Brooks gives us an excellent definition of this depravity.

> By physical depravity is meant the impairment of the substance of the mind or body resulting from the fall. This may be called the weakness or disease of our nature from which proceed many errors of judgment and consequent blunders in the outer life, neither of which involves a bias toward evil—a bent toward selfishness—the inclination to what is inconsistent with love to God or man.[16]

Can this depraved body be called sinful? Wesley does not think so. He says the expression is "deeply ambiguous," and there is no authority in the Scriptures for it. "For no body or matter of any kind can be sinful."[17] However, this body is depraved and disordered, and so is less than it would have been had man not fallen.

This means that the desires and appetites of the body are set in a weakened and debased body. Those physical appetites in themselves cannot be sinful nor would they be expected to be normal. "Weakness, sickness, and disorders of a thousand kinds, are" the body's "natural attendants."[18] Natural desires and appetites of the body may be strongly solicited to indulge themselves, and still not be sin.[19] The natural appetites of sense—for food, pleasant smells—and even the sex desire, can be indulged without sin, although they do not become the spring for our happiness.[20]

Wesley looked upon the body as being "brittle" and "shattered."[21] It needed proper care so it could be of best use to the spirit.[22] It is a "clog" to the soul and hinders its operations. Because of this it is as natural to "mistake as to breathe."[23]

Lack of Knowledge

Many of one's mistakes grow out of his lack of knowledge. That is why the sins of infirmity are sometimes called sins of ignorance. Man is not perfect in knowledge. He is not free from ignorance, nor is man infallible.[24] It is possible to increase knowledge, and one should when he can, especially when that ignorance is causing spiritual darkness.[25] But man has only a small share of the knowledge in his present state. This lack is permitted to keep down pride and help us to depend on God.[26] He calls our apprehensions "confused" and "inaccurate."[27]

> To know what holiness has not done, and knowing this, be governed by these facts without becoming unsettled when these limitations are encountered and felt, will make for happiness and contentment in a holy life.[28]

Sangster criticizes Wesley's teaching on sanctification because, if one believes he is pure, he might cover up some unseen sin in the life. "No man knows what is in him."[29] Wesley could say the same thing, only he believed that an honest seeker could be convicted of the great evil within and by faith could have it removed. When one realizes the limitation of knowledge and the weakness of man, even after full holiness, there should be little danger of his shielding sin within himself.

Wandering Thoughts

Wesley has a sermon on "Wandering Thoughts."[30] Men who had professed full cleansing were bothered by such thoughts and wondered if they still had sin. Wesley proceeds to clarify the truth. He is sure that one can be freed from evil thoughts. He distinguishes between evil thoughts and thoughts of evil. One could think about some evil things without being sinful, but evil or sinful thoughts were to be put away.[31]

Generally there are two kinds of wandering thoughts—those that wander from God, and those that wander from the particular point at hand. The first kind is that of sinners whose thoughts constantly wander away from God. It is the natural thing for every man to do, because by nature he is "without God in the world." Worse yet, they may become angry, malicious, revengeful, and unbelieving thoughts. The other kind are those that wander away from the present subject, but do not leave God out or fight against him.[32]

What are some of the innocent wandering thoughts? There are those that arise out of weakness of the body or because of disease. This "corruptible body" can "press down the soul, and cause it to muse about many things." When one is asleep, he may dream, and he cannot be the master of his thoughts at that time. Who can then prevent them from "wandering from pole to pole?" Even when one is half awake, or half asleep, or when he is dull and languid, he cannot pursue thought. By the imagination and a "motion of the spirits" or a "vibration of the nerves," one can be carried to and fro in his thoughts.[33]

Causes of such thoughts can come from without. Satan is able to distract our thoughts. He may harass and perplex, and he may inject a thousand thoughts. Innocent outward objects may distract, take our attention and lead us away from the subject at hand.[34]

> If they arise from an infirm constitution, or from some accidental weakness or distemper, they are as innocent as it is to have a weak constitution, or a distempered body. And surely no one doubts but a bad state of nerves, a fever of any kind, and either a transient or a lasting delirium, may consist with perfect innocence. And if they should arise in a soul which is united to a healthful body, either from the natural union between the body and soul, or from any of ten thousand changes which may occur in those organs of the body that minister to thought:—in any of these cases they are as perfectly innocent as the causes from which they spring.[35]

Mistakes

Out of the limitations occasioned by a weakened body and mind, and out of the ignorance due to a lack of knowledge, many mistakes will come. These mistakes indeed are "almost an unavoidable consequence of" ignorance. Those who "know in part" are ever "liable to err, touching the things which they know not." The children of God do not mistake concerning the things essential to salvation, but in those things that are "unessential to salvation they do err, and that frequently." One mistake leads to another, so that a person could believe an action to be good when it is evil, or evil when it is good. And such mistakes may lead to wrong judgments concerning men's characters.[36]

Wesley warns against classifying sins as infirmity. Some men are inclined to excuse some special sin of theirs as an infirmity but, unless such persons repent, they shall, with their "infirmities, go quick to hell!" Then Wesley makes clear that the infirmities he means are not only those classified as "bodily infirmities," but also "those inward or outward imperfections which are not of a moral nature."[37]

Weaknesses and infirmities are not sins. Wesley cannot see how Paul could take "pleasure in weaknesses," nor how they could make him strong if they were sins. One cannot glory in "anger, or pride, or lust."[38]

Since man is in a fallen state, he can no longer "avoid falling into innumerable mistakes; consequently, he cannot always avoid wrong affections; neither can he always think, speak, and act right."

> The highest perfection which man can attain, while the soul dwells in the body, does not exclude ignorance, and error, and a thousand other infirmities. Now from wrong judgments, wrong words and actions will often necessarily flow: and in some cases, wrong affections also may spring from the same source. I may judge wrong of you; I may think more or less highly of you than I ought to think; and this mistake in my judgment, may not only occasion something wrong in my behavior, but it may still have a deeper effect; it may occasion something wrong in my affection. From a wrong apprehension, I may love and esteem you either more or less than I ought. Nor can I be freed from a liableness to such a mistake, while I remain in a corruptible body. A thousand infirmities, in consequence of this, will attend my spirit, till it returns to God who gave it.[39]

Sin and Temptation

Temptation itself is not sin, nor does one need to be sinful to suffer temptation. This is proved by the experience of Christ himself who was tempted, yet was not sinful. There is no freedom from such in this life.[40] Satan is in the world and there is no deliverance from him. He will "inject unbelieving, or blasphemous, repining thoughts." He will suggest that God does not rule, or govern aright. "He will endeavor to stir up the heart against God, to renew our natural enmity against him."[41]

Besides Satan there are many causes of temptation for the one who is perfect in love. There is the weakened and infirm body which limits the soul. There is the wicked world with all its enemies of God. There are regenerated persons who still have evil tempers. And there are sanctified individuals who "still have infirmities enough to try all the grace that God has given us."[42]

> One may start, tremble, change color, or be otherwise disordered in body, while the soul is calmly stayed on God, and remains in perfect peace. Nay, the mind itself may be deeply distressed, may be exceeding sorrowful, may be perplexed and pressed down by heaviness and anguish, even to agony, while the heart cleaves to God by perfect love, and the will is wholly resigned to him.[43]

Wesley is attempting to draw a line between the purely physical and mental part of man's constitution, which is of a non-moral nature, and the moral nature centered in the spirit. This line of distinction is not easy to find and, as Dr. Peck suggests, it is perhaps left obscure so that we may exercise "our faculties of moral discrimination."[44] Human desires and passions are "wholly void of moral character" in themselves, and can become instruments of sin only when temptation finds concurrence within the heart.[45] Temptation resisted, even though it be greatly strengthened by our weakened humanity, can be a means of growth in faith and holiness.[46]

Infirmity and Perfect Love

That infirmity is not sinful and, therefore, not inconsistent with Wesley's idea of perfect love has been made clear. The having a corruptible body does not make perfect love impossible.[47] Wesley warned against including imaginary ingredients in the concept of perfection which are not according to Scripture. "Pure love reigning alone in the heart and life—this is the whole of Scriptural perfection."[48] It was impossible for Wesley to see how infirmities, mistakes, a weak and disordered body, wandering thoughts, distressed mind or temptation were in any wise contrary to his concept of perfect love.

He was aware that entire sanctification was not full perfection. He saw that God's goal for man was not that of Adamic perfection, but it was a perfection arrived at by the law of love. Perfection, then was reaching the place of perfect love to God. He did not think too many reached even this kind of perfection, but he believed men could by the grace of God reach this goal, so he ever held out the hope. It is clear that anything in man's conduct that was consistent with perfect love, and yet short of a higher perfection, is not sin. It would be something that could not be avoided, even by the grace of God; therefore, it should not be called sin.

However, Wesley makes clear that anything short of fulfillment of the perfect law, even though it was consistent with perfect love, needed the atonement of Christ. Turner thinks Wesley was inconsistent in thinking these "sins of ignorance" needed forgiveness.[49] But, when one remembers that Wesley saw man apart from Christ and his grace as deserving of punishment, even before any willful sin, he can more easily see that Wesley is only consistent with his own views when he believes that sins of infirmity need the atonement of Christ.[50] Even these mistakes cannot bear the "rigors of God's justice."

The Restored Image of God

Wesley always kept in mind that which man had by creation, and what he had lost in the fall. He believed that man was created in the "Natural" and "Moral Image of God," and that he lost that image in the fall. He taught that all that was lost in Adam could be regained in Christ. In fact man could regain infinitely more than he lost.[51]

Through prevenient grace the natural image is partly restored. Man is allowed to live and propagate a race, and everyone at birth is a recipient of that grace. Through that grace one can improve himself in life, see his sinfulness, repent and believe the gospel. No matter how "good" a man may become there is no renewal of the moral image until he is "born again." Until then he is completely empty of spiritual life and true holiness. Regeneration is the renewal of that image of God in man which becomes the treasure that is in the "earthen vessel."[52]

However, regeneration does not complete that renewal; it is only the beginning. Man now has life, the essence of that moral image, and he is "*truly,* yet not *entirely* renewed." He is still sinful.[53] The full renewal and restoration to the image of God is accomplished in entire sanctification. "It is the renewal of the heart in the whole image of God, the full likeness of him that created it."[54] This comes when the heart is made perfect in love.

But man is not completely restored until the resurrection. It is then he shall be freed from the corruptible body when all limitation of an earthly life is removed.[55] Since knowledge was a part of that original natural image of God, as well as other perfect qualities, man's fullest restoration is yet to come. In this life we cannot attain unto the perfection of Adam, whose understanding was clear and whose affections were regular.[56] But in the resurrection that full glory shall be ours.

For the wicked who turn not to God there is no restoration except what would come to them through prevenient grace. Only those who live with God now can live with him hereafter.[57] So only those men who by grace return to God will be restored to the image of God. For them all the sin derived from Adam and from their own choices is removed. All the punishment that came upon them for the sin of Adam end in the resurrection. All else that has suffered because of the fall will be restored. The earth will be renewed, and even the brutes will be restored.[58] Man because he sinned will be far richer than if sin had never entered the world. And all this glory is because of the atonement in Jesus Christ.

Endnotes

1. *Works*, VII, 37.
2. *Ibid.*, I, 355.
3. *Ibid.*, II, 172.
4. *Ibid.*, I, 72.

5. *Ibid.*, VI, 500-501.
6. Lindstrom, *op. cit.,* 147.
7. Fletcher, *op. cit.,* II, 493.
8. Daniel Steele, *Love Enthroned*, New York: Phillips and Hunt, 1881, 83-85. (Now available from Schmul Publishing Co., Nicholasville, KY.)
9. *Works*, II, 479.
10. Harry Jessop, *Foundations of Doctrine*, Chicago: Chicago Evangelistic Institute, 1938, 160. (Now available from Schmul Publishing Co., Nicholasville, KY.)
11. Henry Brockett, *Scriptural Freedom from Sin*, Kansas City: Kingshiway Press, 1941, 54. (Now available from Schmul Publishing Co., Nicholasville, KY.)
12. *Works*, II, 33-34.
13. *Ibid.*, 53.
14. *Ibid.*, 73.
15. *Ibid.*, 480.
16. John Brooks, *Scriptural Sanctification*, Nashville: Publishing House of the M. E. Church, South, 1899, 15.
17. *Works*, II, 172.
18. *Ibid.*, 213.
19. Fletcher, *op. cit.,* II, 530.
20. *Works*, VI, 503.
21. *Ibid.*, II, 479; VI, 515.
22. *Ibid.*, 270-272.
23. *Ibid.*, VI, 513.
24. *Ibid.*, 489.
25. *Ibid.*, I, 417
26. *Ibid.*, II, 73. See Sermon, "*The Imperfection of Human Knowledge*," 116-125. Wesley had little confidence in man's ability to know much.
27. *Ibid.*, 214.
28. T. M. Anderson, *After Holiness, What?,* Kansas City: Nazarene Publishing House, 1929, 33. (Now available from Schmul Publishing Co., Nicholasville, KY.)
29. Sangster, *op. cit.*, 135, 160.
30. *Works*, I, 370-376.
31. *Ibid.*, I, 365.
32. *Ibid.*, 370-371.
33. *Ibid.,* 372.
34. *Ibid.*, 373.
35. *Ibid.*, 374.

36. *Ibid.*, 356.
37. *Ibid.*, 357.
38. *Ibid.*, 363.
39. *Ibid.*, II, 168.
40. *Ibid.*, I, 358.
41. *Ibid.*, 421-422.
42. *Ibid.*, II, 214-215.
43. *Ibid.*, VI, 503.
44. George Peck, *Christian Perfection*, New York: Lane and Scott, 1850, 436-437. (Now available from Schmul Publishing Co., Nicholasville, KY.)
45. R. S. Foster, *Christian Purity*, New York: Eaton and Mains, 1897, 68-69.
46. *Works*, I, 423-424.
47. *Ibid.*, II, 169.
48. *Ibid.*, VI, 504.
49. Turner, *op. cit.*, 238.
50. *Works*, VI, 500-501.
51. *Ibid.*, II, 37.
52. *Ibid.*, 479.
53. *Ibid.*, I, 112, 116.
54. *Ibid.*, II, 222; VI, 530.
55. *Ibid.*, 73.
56. *Ibid.*, 168.
57. *Ibid.*, VI, 136-137.
58. *Ibid.*, II, 54.

Chapter 10

The Influence of Wesley's View

IN THE INTRODUCTION OF this book there was a brief indication of the influence of Wesley as a man and a religious leader. He wrote widely, and his ideas have been recognized in many fields of thought. Usually he is recognized more as a greater administrator and evangelist than a theologian. That he was a theologian should not be doubted when one sees the many controversies into which he was plunged. That his ideas did influence men in his century and the century following cannot be doubted. To what extent his thinking influenced his own and following generations is harder to determine.

In this chapter we will deal only with the influence that Wesley's view of sin had on others. In a day when the Wesleyan heritage is highly prized by many, it will be interesting to see how much of Wesley's concept of sin has been retained by those who prize that heritage. This effort will be confined to an observation of the teaching on sin as found in the successors to Wesley. Their ideas, compared to Wesley's, will give a general idea how well the founder has been followed in his concept of sin.

The Summary of Wesley's Concept

There are four areas in Wesley's thought that should especially be kept in mind as we make these comparisons, The first is his concept of original man and the fall. Wesley firmly believed in the historicity of the Genesis account of the creation of the first pair in original righteousness and of their consequent fall. The original perfection of man lost in the fall is for Wesley the background for the "restored image" in salvation.

A second basic fact for Wesley was that "in Adam all die." Adam propagates children in his own likeness, so that the race is born devoid of the image of God. Since Adam was head and representative of the race all his descendants are born under the curse of sin and are justly liable to the punishments for the original sin. The loss of God's image and the consequent punishments account for the present wicked state of mankind.

For the third basic factor in Wesley's thought we turn to the two concepts of the nature of man by birth and prevenient grace. Wesley held these two ideas in tension. Man by nature is totally corrupt and incapable of any good, but by grace all men are restored to an ability to choose and are given the divine light, called conscience. Yet Wesley could never look upon man as being good "by nature" even after he begins to use the grace afforded him.

The fourth area in which we shall compare Wesley's thoughts with others is in his distinctions as to the nature of sin. His threefold definition of sin as willful sin, as the principle of sin and as infirmity must be kept in mind. For him these distinctions were of vital importance in his teaching of Christian perfection.

The Development of Wesley's Views

That Wesley did come to a reformed conception of justification by faith in the year 1738 cannot be doubted. This year did mark a change in his concept as to how salvation is attained, although it did not change his view that holiness is the essence of religion and that it should be the goal in the seeking of salvation. When he discovered by experience that justification was by faith, and instantaneous, it was only a matter of time until he saw that the goal, or holiness, was also by faith and could be attained instantaneously. Although his basic conception of holiness, or full salvation, did not change from the time he was at Oxford, there was a development in his varied concepts as to how and when attained and as to the remaining infirmities after the experience. A careful reading of his *Plain Account of Christian Perfection* will reveal this.

During this development of his thinking on salvation some change occurred in his concept of sin. At the time of his conversion, influenced by his previous experiences with the Indians, his belief in the utter corruption of the race by Adam's sin was strengthened. It was in his defense of the doctrine of Christian perfection, however, that he clarified the distinction between the sins of infirmity and the willful sins, and between the inbred sin and the remaining infirmities. There is no clear evidence that there was any other change in his concept of sin over the period of his long life.

Wesley has nevertheless been accused of changing his conception of the total depravity of man by nature. In his own day such an accusation was made.[1] His emphasis on prevenient grace, free choice and the necessity of repentance gave many, especially Calvinists, occasion to think that he allowed man some natural ability to cooperate with God in his salvation. Wheeler in his book on the *Twenty-Five Articles of the Methodist Episcopal Church* is very sure that Wesley changed his view regarding imputed guilt.[2] The only evidence that is given to show that such a change occurred is the omission by Wesley, in the drafting of the Twenty-Four Articles, of parts in the Ninth Article of the Thirty-Nine dealing with original guilt.[3] Wheeler notes that Wesley omits the word "fault," and the phrase concerning "flesh" that "it deserveth God's wrath and damnation." He recognizes that Pope endorses the Ninth Article of the English Church and that he claims that the Methodist Church also accepts it.

> This cannot be true of Methodism in general. Wesley purposely rejected it when he abridged the Article for the use of the American Methodists, and as has been seen in the above quotations, it is rejected by Fletcher, Watson, and the American Methodist divines.[4]

Whedon, one of the American Methodist divines, has this to say:

> Wesley rejects the doctrine of our personal desert of damnation here affirmed, for the very good reason that it contradicts our intuitive sense of right and justice. That rejection removes a contradiction to the moral sense and to common sense from theology. Great were Wesley's logical powers; greater his administrative powers; but greatest of all his intuitive powers... And undoubtedly the moment when he prepared these Twenty-Four Articles was, if any moment of his life, the crisis when he looked at pure, absolute truth.[5]

John Miley, who quotes favorably from the above, adds another word from Whedon that Wesley's revision is the supreme authority canceling the earlier writings of Wesley that were "doctrinally contrary to this Article." "In his *Southern Review,* 1876, Dr. Bledsoe ably discussed the doctrinal significance of the change in this article, and maintained as a sure implication, that in his later years, Wesley repudiated his earlier views of original sin."[6]

Wheeler further believes that Wesley also changed his views about "works before justification" because he left out of the Twenty-Four Articles the one on "Works Before Justification." He thinks Wesley was "too broad-minded and too wise" to make these kind of works to "have the nature of sin," and to make such belief an article of religion.[7] To this Lee agrees. He thinks Wesley looked upon works proceeding from grace in a different light when he was older.[8] Miley holds that this revision is the doctrine of the Methodist Episcopal Church, and they should have changed the second article to have been consistent. This second article leaves the words, "original guilt," in the revision. He says it was an oversight.[9]

Are these American Methodists reading into Wesley what they want there, or did Wesley change his view? They admitted that Pope, an English Methodist, disagreed with them, but say that Fletcher and Watson agree. However, we have already noted in this book that Watson held to original guilt, in the sense that Wesley did.[10] Fletcher makes very clear that mankind is guilty of Adam's sin. "We may then justly infer, from the sufferings and death of still-born or new-born children, that man is totally degenerate, and liable to destruction, even from his mother's womb."[11]

Fletcher confesses in 1771, when Wesley was sixty-eight years old, that he has heard Wesley for sixteen years frequently and that "upon every proper occasion," he steadily maintains "the total fall of man in Adam." "The deepest expressions that ever struck my ears on the melancholy subject of our natural depravity and helplessness are those which dropped from his lips."[12]

> But you possibly imagine, sir, that he has lately changed his doctrine, and adopted a new system. If you do, you are under a very great mistake; and to convince you of it, permit me to conclude this letter by a paragraph of one which I received from him last spring:

> "I always did (for between these thirty and forty years) clearly assert the total fall of man, and his utter inability to do any good of himself; the absolute necessity of the grace and Spirit of God to raise even a good thought or desire in our hearts... And who is there in England that has asserted these things more strongly and steadily than I have done."[13]

When one remembers that Wesley revised the Articles less than five years after this letter, it is more difficult to believe he changed his opinion.

Why then do these American Methodists think Wesley changed? It is best answered by noting their failure to hold in proper tension what man is by nature and what he is by grace. To say that because Christ died man is not born guilty does not explain Wesley. By nature, or birth, man is guilty of original sin. By grace, the guilt is taken away. Cell believes that Wesley taught total depravity. "It could not be blacker."[14] But, he says, this concept "must never be divorced from his doctrine of prevenient grace."[15] Why then did he omit parts of the Thirty-nine Articles? It would seem for the purpose of brevity and of eliminating Calvinistic elements.[16] Further reasons for the American Methodist attitude will be given later.

Wesley's Influence in the Nineteenth Century

For the Methodists who claimed to follow Wesley, his writings became the primary source of doctrine along with Fletcher's writings and the Bible.[17] The British Wesleyans were close followers of Wesley. Watson and Pope are the leading English Methodist theologians. It was noted above that Watson and Pope stood with Wesley on the point of original guilt. Of course it is understood that this guilt is not personal, only a liability to punishment. Pope insists that not only St. Paul taught original guilt, but also Christ, and that the teaching pervades the Scriptures.[18]

Pope further states that Wesley's treatise on original sin is one of the "most faithful and stern reflections of the Scriptural doctrine in our language."[19] He agrees with Wesley, Fletcher and Watson. He thinks their position on sin is the best because it is in harmony with all the facts. The doctrine "omits nothing, evades nothing, softens nothing."[20]

From this evidence there is no indication that the English Methodists of the Nineteenth Century differed from Wesley's view.

The picture is a bit different for the American Methodists. As noted above they did differ on the concept of original guilt although they wanted to think that Wesley had changed. Foster is more true to the facts when he admits that Wesley and Watson held to guilt of a kind. However, he objects to considering another guilty for someone else's sin. Guilt cannot be hereditary.[21] Bishop Foster, who wrote in the latter part of the Nineteenth Century, sums up quite well the American variation from Wesley. He accepts that man is fallen, but rejects the idea of guilt connected with this corruption.[22] Punishment can only be for the personal offender, and punishment cannot be inflicted on another who did not commit the sin. Those sufferings as a result of another's sin cannot be termed punishment.[23]

Why did the American Methodists take this trend away from the position of Wesley? These men were faced with strong Calvinistic opposition. They developed a theory of "gracious ability" on the basis of prevenient grace.[24]

> American Methodism did not abide by its own theological heritage. It increasingly traced the uniqueness of its theological position, not to the stress on the universally-personal relevance of redemptive grace, but simply to a stress on the person's intrinsic, absolute freedom of contrary choice.[25]

This rejection of original guilt, and the assimilation of certain nonevangelical developments in philosophical theology became a "major aspect of the prolegomena to twentieth century American Methodist's strong championship of the Ritschlian and Personalistic views of man and the religious life."[26] In this "rejection of original guilt" the American Methodists thought they were following Wesley. Although Wesley did not go all the way with the Augustinian concept, which made original guilt personal, he did retain the idea of guilt as a liability to punishment. "The repudiation, therefore, by the majority of Methodist ministers" (and this includes the English by the end of the Nineteenth Century) "of the doctrine of total depravity in its extreme Augustinian forms is one of the marks of the times, and is a necessary result of the triumph of Arminianism."[27] In this quote I would question only the word "necessary."

Except for this one divergence, it is safe to say that the Nineteenth-Century Methodists maintained the four basic points in Wesley's concept of sin. The loss of original perfection, the corruption of all human nature by the fall, the restoration through prevenient grace and the three-fold definition of sin were faithfully held in Methodist circles almost to the close of the Nineteenth Century.

Wesley and the Twentieth Century

Wesley's teachings, as they approach the Twentieth Century, encounter several factors that cause a greater repudiation on the part of Methodists. The theory of evolution would strike a blow at Wesley's concept of original man and his fall. Tennant, who had influence on Methodists though not a Methodist himself, is one theologian who held with Wesley that sin in its proper sense is voluntary. But he does reject any idea of sinfulness in man's nature because of his acceptance of the Darwinian theory.[28] Sangster is in this same class.[29]

Biblical criticism became another battleground for Wesley's views since he had based his opinion upon the historicity of the account of the fall in the Scriptures. On this basis it now became easy to challenge Wesley's concept of an historical fall. For example, Lee thinks if Wesley lived today he might not have accepted the dogma of the fall.[30] However, Wesley never allowed himself to question the authority of the Scriptures.

Twentieth-Century concepts of the basic dignity of man, of the fatherhood of God and the brotherhood of man, strike a blow at Wesley's concept of fallen nature. The attempt to build a better social order without first a radical change in the individual runs counter to Wesley's view. Personalism, humanism, and liberalism may find some elements in Wesley that are similar, but they do not agree with Wesley's concept of sin.

Most Methodists like to feel that they are following Wesley, but it is easy to pick out those points in him that one likes, and discard the rest, or reinterpret them. Probably no Methodist is a complete follower of

Wesley. Who of modern Methodists most nearly follow Wesley in his concept of sin? There will be two contrasting groups—those who closely follow his concept and those who either repudiate it or ignore it. Many others could be classified all the way between the extremes.

The Holiness Groups

As some Methodists moved away from the traditional Wesleyan view on sin and holiness, others formed groups to maintain what they considered to be the original emphasis. During the camp meetings of the latter part of the Nineteenth Century, those interested in the doctrine and experience of holiness banded together and formed the National Association for the Promotion of Holiness in 1866. Before this the Wesleyan Methodist Connection was organized in 1843. The Free Methodist Church began in 1860. Toward the close of the century the Church of the Nazarene was organized from many independent holiness churches.

Most of these were Methodists who felt that the Methodist churches were deviating from Wesley and who wanted to conserve his doctrinal emphases. These above groups are not to be confused with the Pentecostal groups who arose later and who have also used the term *holiness*. These latter groups have emphasized the "gifts of Pentecost" but have no special interest in the Wesleyan doctrines.

The holiness groups have attempted to maintain Wesley's doctrines of justification by faith, regeneration, and sanctification. How well they have followed Wesley in other areas is not considered here. They lay claim to the term *Wesleyanism* and believe they are truly Arminian. It is a form of "Wesleyan Arminianism."[31]

There have been a number of theologians who have spoken for these groups during the last fifty years [1957-*ed.*] three of whom were A. M. Hills, Joseph Smith and Orton Wiley. Some of these have followed the English theologians more closely and others the American, but all claim to follow Wesley. None of them raise any question concerning Wesley's idea of original man and his fall into sin. The historicity of the Genesis account is not rejected by any of them.[32] They all maintain the loss of original perfection.

Among these men there is the same divergence of view as to the doctrine of original guilt, as was found between the English and American Methodists in the Nineteenth Century. A.M. Hills follows Miley and Foster more closely in accepting fallen man as still being able to choose right or wrong and in no sense guilty of Adam's sin.[33] He does not give as great a place to prevenient grace as does Wesley.[34] On the other hand Wiley follows Watson and Pope more closely, and more closely follows Wesley in the concepts of original guilt and prevenient grace.[35]

Concerning the distinctions in the nature of sin, all of the holiness writers have been careful to observe Wesley's three-fold classification. Teaching holiness as a possible experience in this life, they of necessity must make these distinctions.[36] One can conclude that those Wesleyans who follow the thought of Wiley also follow Wesley in his concept of sin. Those who follow Hills or Miley follow Wesley except in the idea of the guilt and penalty of original sin. It is safe to say that, in general, the holiness groups, whether as separate churches, or as a small part of the Methodist Church, do retain closely Wesley's concept of sin. They follow very well the Nineteenth Century Methodists in the doctrine of sin.

The Methodist Church

That many modem Methodists value highly the heritage of Wesley and try to follow him in many ways cannot be doubted. Piette thinks they have retained the element of Christian experience as found in Wesley.[37] Wesley's emphasis upon the social aspects of the gospel has been emphasized and given a large place in modern Methodism. Some see that the emphasis of Wesley upon love laid the foundation for the fatherhood of God and the brotherhood of man.[38] Present day stress on education and discipline for morality are traced back to Wesley.[39]

The question we must face now is regarding Wesley's concept of sin. Do Methodists in general still follow Wesley in their doctrine of sin? "The unitive element in Methodism is much more functional than it is dogmatic."[40] Methodists do not claim to be a doctrinal church. Any attempt to reduce their sources of doctrine to a confession of faith has resulted in failure.[41] Because of this fact it is difficult to discover just what Methodists believe.

That there is in modern Methodism that which deviates almost completely from Wesley's concept of sin is very evident. It would be clear that those who accept the theory of evolution would consider Wesley's view of original righteousness and the fall too naive. Others because of Biblical criticism have rejected the dogma of the fall. Knudson could not see that there was any place, anymore, for the Augustinian concept of sin.[42] He, along with Tennant and Sangster, could not believe a person to be sinful until a wrong choice was made.[43] Any depravity before that choice could not be of a sinful nature. This opinion rejects any idea of an original righteousness lost in a fall of the first parents. Nor could it accept any idea of an original guilt or sinful depravity that is transmitted from Adam to the race.

What about the nature of man and prevenient grace? Much has been said about the dignity of man, and the spark of divinity in him.[44] Nature by some is not considered evil.[45] There has been a Methodist susceptibility to a "somewhat Pelagian doctrine of moral agency."[46] It is claimed by William Sperry that Methodism shared in the "vote of confidence" in man by liberalism.[47] This optimistic side to human nature is associated with the grace of God.[48] A quote from *Major Methodist Belief* is as follows:

> Man is by nature capable of responding to the *beautiful.* He can love the *truth* and repudiate errors. And he can seek that absolute *righteousness* which comes only from loyal service to the one true God. In his natural state these capacities are both undeveloped and even twisted by his pride and pettiness. But they are always there just the same. And because of these things man is a creature of dignity.[49]

In the youth quarterly for the Sunday School, this statement appears: "The nature God has given us is good. Only our misuse of it is evil."[50] In a broad sense Wesley could accept this statement, but only as true of the original nature given to Adam and his misuse of it. Because Adam sinned, all human nature is now evil before there is any use of it by individuals. To see good in human nature as it now is would be to see good through prevenient grace. There is for Wesley no goodness from any other source.

Following up the consequences of the above attitude on sin and the nature of man, it becomes very evident that there is no need for Wesley's three-fold distinction in the nature of sin. Sangster and Knudson agree in making sin of one nature—wrong moral choice. This takes away the sinfulness in man's disordered nature. This nature is unfortunate but cannot be sinful. And with only one kind of sin there will be no emphasis upon infirmities as sin. Thus it seems that for those who hold the above attitudes, Wesley's concept of sin is quite completely set aside. How deeply do these attitudes go in Methodism? Cell makes the following comment.

> The loss of the original Wesleyan perspective of truth-values in the gospel and the radical dislocation of emphasis due to Calvinistic controversies, the reception into Methodist theology within the last fifty years of the historical and higher criticism of Scripture and Dogma, and the radical shift from evangelical to humanist principles in much recent Methodist religious thought has given rise to such humanist accommodations as that total depravity in not an essentially Methodist doctrine, or that Methodism is the first great religious revival based on a libertarian theology. These humanist accommodations do indeed represent the temper of much present-day Methodist theology, but if imputed to John Wesley, they are pure fiction.[51]

It is only fair to say that this above extreme position on sin as held by some Methodists cannot be imputed even to a majority in this church. Where the "holiness" Methodists have maintained without much exception the same view as Wesley on sin, this other group has largely rejected that view. The only likeness to Wesley is in their concept of sin as "wrong moral choice." Wesley held that only the "voluntary" sin could separate from God.

Most Methodists will be found somewhere between these two extreme views on sin. Even for the "holiness" groups it is impossible to go all the way with Wesley's concept of original perfection in nature, or his concept of Adam's guilt being passed on to all his posterity. Nor is it possible for those of the other extreme to reject all of Wesley's concept of a disordered and fallen nature in man.

William Hordern, an instructor at Swarthmore College, who accepts the basic idea of evolution and rejects the historicity of the Genesis account, thinks the idea of the fall was laughed at too quickly. There is a return to that concept today.[52] While many are returning to the idea of the fall, there are some who never "laughed at" the idea. One Methodist theologian who has maintained this concept of the fall is Edwin Lewis. Since 1916 he has been instructor in theology at Drew Theological Seminary, and has written many books. Dr. Lewis would represent a mediating view between the two extremes.

Dr. Lewis would not hold as Wesley did that Adam possessed an original righteousness which he lost when he fell. He would see the Genesis account more as a picture of what happens in every man, rather than an actual, historical happening at the origin of the human race. This account has great meaning for Lewis, but not in the same way as it did for Wesley.[53]

Although Dr. Lewis would not see the transmission of sin as a penal consequence of Adam's sin, he would see sinfulness in man as an hereditary thing.[54]

> It is so patent that man perpetually produces a kingdom of evil, and the man who produces evil has evil at the heart of him. He starts with a moral blight, and the blight manifests itself in the work of his hands. Augustine, with all his exaggeration, was much nearer the truth about man than was Pelagius.[55]

For Lewis, as it was for Wesley, this "moral tragedy" is evident everywhere. The only way to account for the "spectacle of human evil which everywhere meets the eye" is to recognize it as "the fruit of a root nourished from within the very depths of human nature itself."[56] The sinfulness precedes the sinning for the "first sin in every person reveals a nature sinful already."[57]

With Wesley, Lewis sees that this doctrine of sin is revealed in the Scriptures, and that it is basic to the whole plan of salvation.[58] This salvation comes because of God's grace freely bestowed upon man.[59] At this point Lewis and Wesley meet in a similar conception of man's fallen nature and of God's free grace. Man is under God's wrath because of his nature, but he has grace from God's free will.[60]

Lewis also makes a distinction between the act of sin, as a choice, and the sinfulness of the nature. "The real 'Fall' is always inward. Every 'Fall' takes place within before its results are manifest without."[61] Furthermore, he recognizes a difference between sins that are expressed in action, and those that are not so expressed. Also he sees a kind of action "whose real intent was not wrong, but which in the light of all their devastating results must be called wrong—sins of human frailty."[62] In these distinctions one can see a likeness to Wesley's three-fold definition of voluntary sins, the principle of sin and sins of infirmity.

It can be concluded that Dr. Lewis is nearer to Wesley than to those who gave a "vote of confidence" to human nature. His essential divergence from Wesley's view is at the point of original perfection, and the kind of fall attributed to a first man. Lewis would not accept the theory of original guilt, but he does place man under divine condemnation for his nature. He would, however, agree with Wesley on the important basic ideas concerning sin.

In view of the mediating position which Lewis represents, and in view of the fact that there is a contemporary return to the doctrine of original sin, it can be said that Wesley's concept of sin still has a place in Christian theology. There will be some points in his view that reflect the concepts of his day, and which will not be enduring. However, since Wesley had such a high regard for the Scriptures and since he was a close student of human nature, the basic and fundamental ideas in his concept of sin must needs be enduring. These basic ideas may be expressed in a different manner, but the underlying truths will live. They are well summed up in Wesley's own words:

> Keep to the plain, old faith, "once delivered to the saints," and delivered by the Spirit of God to our hearts. Know your disease! Know your cure! Ye were born in sin: therefore "ye must be born again," born of God. By nature ye are wholly corrupted: by grace ye shall be wholly renewed. In Adam ye all died: in the second Adam, in Christ, ye all are made alive."[63]

Endnotes

1. Fletcher, *op. cit.*, I, 19.
2. Wheeler, *op. cit.*, 184. The Twenty-four Articles drafted by Wesley were increased to twenty-five in America.
3. *Ibid.*, 23.
4. *Ibid.*, 184-185.
5. Whedon, *Methodist Quarterly Review*, 1882, 365, quoted from Miley, *op. cit.*, II, 525.
6. Miley, *op. cit.*, II, 525, footnote.
7. Wheeler, *op. cit.*, 25-26.
8. Lee, *op. cit.,* 171.
9. Miley, *op. cit.,* II, 524-525.
10. Watson, *op. cit.*, II, 53.
11. Fletcher, *op. cit.*, II, 263.
12. *Ibid.*, I, 12.
13. *Ibid.*, 19.
14. George Cell, *The Rediscovery of John Wesley*, New York: Henry Holt and Co., 1935, 274.
15. *Ibid.*, 281.
16. Turner, *op. cit.*, 199.
17. Leland Scott, "Methodist Theology in America in the Nineteenth Century," *Religion and Life*, XXV, 89.
18. Pope, *op. cit.*, II, 51.
19. *Ibid.*, 80.
20. *Ibid.*, 82.
21. Foster, *Studies, op. cit.*, II, 180, 238.
22. *Ibid.*, 133.
23. *Ibid.*, 119-120.
24. Scott, *op. cit.*, 90-91.
25. *Ibid.*, 92.
26. *Ibid.*, 94.
27. Townsend, *op. cit.*, I, 53.
28. Tennant, *op. cit.*, 142.
29. Sangster, *op. cit.*, 120.
30. Lee, *op. cit.*, 314.
31. Wiley, *op. cit.*, II, 455-456.
32. Wiley, *op. cit.*, II, 9. A. M. Hills, *Fundamental Christian Theology*, Pasadena:

C. J. Kinne, 1931, I, 326. (Now available from Schmul Publishing Co., Nicholasville, KY.)

33. Hills, *op. cit.*, I, 405-406.
34. *Ibid.*, II, 145-146.
35. Wiley, *op. cit.*, II, 107-109.
36. *Ibid.* 473-474, 507. Hills, *op. cit.*, II, 224-225.
37. Piette, *John Wesley in the Evolution of Protestantism*, New York: Sheed and Ward, 1937, 477.
38. Townsend, *op. cit.*, II, 441-442.
39. Lee, *op. cit.*, 304-308.
40. Scott, *op. cit.*, 98.
41. Piette, *op. cit.,* 477.
42. Albert Knudson, *Basic Issues in Christian Thought*, New York: Abingdon-Cokesbury Press, 1950, 99.
43. *Ibid.*, 119.
44. Townsend, *op. cit.*, II, 435.
45. E. Brightman, *Personalism in Theology*, Boston: University Press, 1943, 83.
46. Scott, *op. cit.*, 98.
47. William Sperry, "Sin and Salvation," *Religion in Life*, XXI, 166.
48. Francis Ensley, *John Wesley Evangelist*, Nashville: Tidings, 1955, 35.
49. Mack Stokes, *Major Methodist Beliefs*, Nashville: The Methodist Publishing House, 1956, 43.
50. Henry Bullock, *Adult Student*, Nashville: The Methodist Publishing House, 1956, XV, No.8, 44.
51. Cell., *op. cit.*, 284.
52. William Hordern, "The Relevance of the Fall," *Religion in Life*, XX, No. 1, New York: Abingdon-Cokesbury Press, 1950-1951, 99.
53. Edwin Lewis, *A Philosophy of the Christian Revelation*, New York: Harper and Brothers, 1940, 104.
54. Edwin Lewis, *A Christian Manifesto*, New York: The Abingdon Press, 1934, 157.
55. Lewis, *Philosophy, op. cit.*, 106.
56. *Ibid.*, 104-105.
57. Lewis, *Manifesto, op. cit.*, 138.
58. *Ibid.*, 132.
59. *Ibid.*, 157.
60. *Ibid.*, 148-149.

61. Edwin Lewis, *The Practice of the Christian Life*, Philadelphia: The Westminster Press, 1942, 49.

62. *Ibid.*, 94.

63. *Works*, I, 399.

Bibliography

The Writings of John Wesley

The Works of the Rev. John Wesley, A.M., with last correction of the author. Third edition, edited by John Emory, seven volumes, New York: The Methodist Book Concern, 1825.

Explanatory Notes Upon the New Testament, London: The Epworth Press, 1948. (Now available from Schmul Publishing Co., Nicholasville, KY.)

Standard Sermons, edited by E.H. Sugden, 2 volumes, London: The Epworth Press, 1921.

The Journal of the Rev. John Wesley, A.M., edited by Nehemiah Curnock, 8 volumes, London: Epworth Press, 1938.

The Letters of the Reverend John Wesley, *A.M.,* edited by John Telford, 8 volumes, London: Epworth Press, 1931.

Poetical Works by Charles and John Wesley. Collected and arranged by G. Osborn, 1868-1872.

A Calm Address to Our American Colonies, edited by Thomas Kepler, Cleveland: World Publishing Co., 1954.

Survey of the Wisdom of God in the Creation, Lancaster, Pa.: Hamilton, 1810.

A Compend of Wesley's Theology, compiled by Robert Burtner and Robert Chiles, New York: Abingdon Press, 1954.

Supplementary Bibliography

Anderson, Tony M., *After Holiness, What?,* Kansas City: Nazarene Publishing House, 1929. (Now available from Schmul Publishing Co., Nicholasville, KY.)

Arminius, James, *Works,* 3 volumes, London: Longman, Hunt, Rees, Orme, Brown, and Green, 1825.

Baldwin, H.A., *Holiness and the Human Element,* Louisville: Pentecostal Publishing Co., 1919. (Now available from Schmul Publishing Co., Nicholasville, KY.)

Bosley, Harold A., *A Firm Faith for Today,* New York: Harper and Brothers Publishers, 1950.

——*Main Issues Confronting Christendom,* New York: Harper and Brothers Publishers, 1948.

Bowen, Marjorie, *Wrestling Jacob,* London: Watts and Co., 1937.

Brailsford, Mabel R., *A Tale of Two Brothers—John and Charles Wesley,* New York: Oxford University Press, 1954.

Bready, J. Wesley, *England: Before and After Wesley,* London: Hodder and Stoughton. Ltd., 1938.

Brightman, Edgar S., *Personalism in Theology,* a symposium, Boston: Boston University Press, 1943.

Brockett, Henry E., *Scriptural Freedom from Sin,* Kansas City: Kingshighway Press, 1941. (Now available from Schmul Publishing Co., Nicholasville, KY.)

Brooks, John R., *Scriptural Sanctification,* Nashville: Publishing House of the M.E. Church, South, 1899.

Bullock, Henry M., *Adult Student,* Vol. 15, No.8, Nashville: The Methodist Publishing House, August, 1956.

Cadman, S. Parks, *The Three Religious Leaders of Oxford and Their Movements,* New York: The Macmillan Co., 1916.

Cairns, David, *The Image of God in Man,* New York: Philosophical Library, 1953.

Cameron, Richard M., *The Rise of Methodism: A Source Book*, New York: Philosophical Library, 1954.

Cannon, William R., *The Theology of John Wesley,* with special reference to the doctrine of justification. (A quite complete bibliography on Wesley.) New York: Abingdon-Cokesbury Press, 1946.

Cell, George Croft, *The Rediscovery of John Wesley,* New York: Henry Holt and Co., 1935.

Clark, Elmer T., *What Happened at Aldersgate?,* Nashville: Methodist Publishing House, 1938.

Clarke, Adam, *Memoirs of the Wesley Family, Collected from Original Documents,* 2 volumes, London: J. Haddon, 1834.

Cooper, Joseph, *The Love Stories of John Wesley, and other Essays.* Boston: The Gorham Press, 1931.

Doughty, William L., *John Wesley: His Conferences and Preachers,* London: The Epworth Press, 1944.

Edwards, Maldwyn, *John Wesley and the Eighteenth Century*, a study of his social and political influence, London: George Allen and Unwin Ltd., 1933.

Ensley, Francis G., *John Wesley Evangelist,* Nashville: Tidings, 1955.

Faulkner, John A., "Wesley's Attitude Toward Luther," *The Lutheran Quarterly,* New Series, Vol. XXXVI, Gettysburg: William B. Hammond, 1906.

——, *Wesley as Sociologist, Theologian, Churchman,* New York: The Methodist Book Concern, 1918.

Fischer, Peti Bohdan, *The Concept of Sin in Luther's Theology,* Chicago: The University of Chicago Libraries, 1945.

Fitchett, W.H., *Wesley and His Century: A Study in Spiritual Forces,* London: Smith, Elder and Co., 1906.

Fletcher, John, *The Works,* 4 volumes, New York: B. Waugh and T. Mason, 1835. (Now available from Schmul Publishing Co., Nicholasville, KY.)

Flew, R. Newton, *The Idea of Perfection in Christian Theology,* London: Oxford University Press, 1934.

Foster, Randolph S., *Christian Purity or The Heritage of Faith,* New York: Eaton and Mains, 1897.

——. *Studies in Theology,* 6 volumes, New York: Eaton and Mains, 1899.

Green, J. Brazier, *John Wesley and William Law,* London: The Epworth Press, 1945.

Haire, Robert, *Wesley's One and Twenty Visits to Ireland: A Short Survey,* London: The Epworth Press, 1947.

Harrison, G. Elsie, *Son to Susanna: The Private Life of John Wesley,* Nashville: Cokesbury Press, 1938.

Hildebrandt, Franz, *From Luther to Wesley,* London: Lutterworth Press, 1951.

Hills, A.M., *Fundamental Christian Theology,* 2 volumes, Pasadena: C.J. Kinne, 1931. (Now available from Schmul Publishing Co., Nicholasville, KY.)

Hordern, William, "The Relevance of the Fall," *Religion in Life,* Vol. XX, No. 1, 99-105, New York: Abingdon-Cokesbury Press, 1950-1951.

Hutton, William H., *John Wesley,* London: Macmillan and Co., 1927.

Jessop, Harry E., *Foundations of Doctrine in Scripture and Experience,* Chicago: Evangelistic Institute, 1938. (Now available from Schmul Publishing Co., Nicholasville, KY.)

Knudson, Albert C., *Basic Issues in Christian Thought,* New York: Abingdon-Cokesbury Press, 1950.

Kroll, Harrison, *The Long Quest,* Philadelphia: The Westminster Press, 1954.

Law, William, *A Serious Call to a Devout and Holy Life,* New York: E.P. Dutton and Co., 1906. (Wesley's edition now available from Schmul Publishing Co., Nicholasville, KY.)

Lecky, William Edward H., *A History of England in the Eighteenth Century,* London: D. Appleton and Co., 1879.

Lee, Umphrey, *John Wesley and Modern Religion,* Nashville: Cokesbury Press, 1936.

Lewis, Edwin, *A Christian Manifesto,* New York: The Abingdon Press, 1934.

——, *A Philosophy of the Christian Revelation,* New York: Harper and Brothers, 1940.

——, *The Practice of the Christian Life,* Philadelphia: The Westminster Press, 1942.

Lindstrom, Harald, *Wesley and Sanctification,* London: The Epworth Press, 1946.

Lipsky, Avram, *John Wesley a Portrait,* New York: Simon and Schuster, 1928.

Luccock, Halford E., and Paul Hutchinson, *The Story of Methodism,* New York: Methodist Book Concern, 1926.

Lunn, Arnold, *John Wesley,* London: Cassell and Company, Ltd., 1929.

Mackintosh, Robert, *Christianity and Sin,* New York: Charles Scribner's Sons, 1914.

McConnell, Francis, *John Wesley,* New York: The Abingdon Press, 1939.

McGiffert, Arthur Cushman, *Protestant Thought Before Kant,* New York: Charles Scribner's Sons, 1936.

Miley, John, *Systematic Theology,* 2 volumes. New York: The Methodist Book Concern, 1892.

Peck, George, *The Scripture Doctrine of Christian Perfection Stated and Defended,* New York: Lane and Scott, 1850.

Piette, Maximin, *John Wesley in the Evolution of Protestantism,* New York: Sheed and Ward, 1937.

Pope, William Burt, *A Compendium of Christian Theology Being Analytical Outlines of a Course of Theological Study, Biblical, Dogmatic, Historical,* 2 volumes, New York: Hunt and Eaton, 1889.

Prince, John W., *Wesley on Religious Education,* New York: The Methodist Book Concern, 1926.

Rattenbury, J. Ernest, *The Conversion of the Wesleys: A Critical Study,* London: The Epworth Press, 1938.

——, *Wesley's Legacy to the World,* Nashville: Cokesbury Press, 1929.

Raymond, Miner, *Systematic Theology,* 3 volumes, Hitchcock and Walden, 1877.

Remsburg, J.E., *Paine and Wesley,* Image Breaker Series.

Rupp, Gordon, *The Righteousness of God*, Luther Studies, New York: Philosophical Library, Inc., 1953.

Sangster, W.E., *The Path to Perfection,* New York: Abingdon-Cokesbury Press, 1943.

Scott, Leland H., "Methodist Theology in America in the Nineteenth Century," *Religion in Life,* Vol. XXV, No. I, 87-98, New York: Abingdon-Cokesbury Press, 1955-1956.

Simon, John S., *John Wesley, The Last Phase,* London: The Epworth Press, 1934.

——, *John Wesley, The Master Builder,* London: The Epworth Press, 1927.

Simpson, W. J. Sparrow, *John Wesley and the Church of England,* New York: The Macmillan Company, 1934.

Smith, H. Shelton, *Changing Conceptions of Original Sin: A Study in American Theology Since 1750,* New York: Charles Scribner's Sons, 1955.

Southey, Robert, *The Life of John Wesley and the Rise and Progress of Methodism,* London: Longman, Brown, Green, and Longmans, 1846.

Spalding, James C., *Recent Restatements of the Doctrines of the Fall and Original Sin,* with special reference to Continental theology, Ann Arbor: University Microfilms, 1950.

Sperry, William, "Sin and Salvation," *Religion in Life,* Vol. XXI, No. 2, 163-206, New York: Abingdon-Cokesbury Press, 1952.

Steele, Daniel, *Love Enthroned,* New York: Phillips and Hunt, 1881. (Now available from Schmul Publishing Co., Nicholasville, KY).

Stokes, Mack B., *Major Methodist Beliefs,* Nashville: The Methodist Publishing House, 1955-1956.

Taylor, Jeremy, *Holy Living and Dying,* London: Henry G. Bohn, 1850.

Taylor, John, *The Scripture-Doctrine of Original Sin Proposed to a Free and Candid Examination.* In three parts including a supplement. Belfast: For John Hay, Bookseller, 1746.

Taylor, Richard S., *A Right Conception of Sin,* Kansas City: Nazarene Publishing House, 1939. (With final revision by the author, now available from Schmul Publishing Co., Nicholasville, KY.)

Tennant, Frederick Robert, *The Concept of Sin,* Cambridge: University Press, 1912.

Thomas à Kempis, *The Imitation of Christ,* New York: J.M. Dent and Sons, Ltd., 1910.

Thompson, David D., *John Wesley as a Social Reformer,* New York: Eaton and Mains, 1898.

Townsend, William J. H.B. Workman, George Eayrs, *A New History of Methodism,* 2 volumes, London: Hodder and Stoughton, 1919.

Trevylyan, Mrs. Kitty, *Diary: A Story of the Times of Whitefield and the Wesleys,* London: T. Nelson and Sons, 1866.

Tucker, Robert L., *The Separation of the Methodists from the Church of England,* New York: The Methodist Book Concern, 1918.

Tyerman, Luke, *The Life and Times of the Rev. John Wesley, A.M.,* 3 volumes, London: Hodder and Stoughton, 1875.

Vulliamy, C.E., *John Wesley*, London: Lowe and Brydone Printers, Ltd., 1931.

Wade, John D., *John Wesley,* New York: Coward-McCann, Inc., 1930.

Warner, Wellman J., *The Wesleyan Movement in the Industrial Revolution,* New York: Longmans, Green and Co., 1930.

Watson, Philip S., *Let God Be God!,* London: The Epworth Press, 1947.

Watson, Richard, *The Life of the Rev. John Wesley, A.M.,* New York: T. Mason and G. Lane, 1839.

——, *Theological Institutes or A View of the Evidence, Doctrines, Morals, and Institutions of Christianity,* 2 volumes, New York: Carlton and Porter, 1857.

Wheeler, Henry, *History and Exposition of the Twenty-Five Articles of Religion of the Methodist Episcopal Church,* New York: Eaton and Mains, 1908.

Whiteley, John H., *Wesley's England: Survey of Eighteenth Century England,* London: The Epworth Press, 1938.

Wiley, H. Orton, *Christian Theology,* 3 volumes. (Contains a very complete bibliography) Kansas City: Nazarene Publishing House, 1941.

Winchester, C.T., *The Life of John Wesley,* New York: The Macmillan Company, 1916.

Wood, J.A., *Purity and Maturity,* Boston: Christian Witness Co., 1899. (Now available from Schmul Publishing Co., Nicholasville, KY.)

Yost, Jesse J., *Plerophona in the Spiritual Experiences of John Wesley,* unpublished M.A. thesis, State University of Iowa, 1922.

Zepp, Arthur C., *Progress After Entire Sanctification,* Chicago: The Christian Witness Co., 1909. (Now available from Schmul Publishing Co., Nicholasville, KY.)

www.ingramcontent.com/pod-product-compliance
Lightning Source LLC
LaVergne TN
LVHW020639100826
845148LV00012B/2254